THE SOUL PURPOSE OF WEALTH

*Stop being a slave to debt,
build wealth
and live life on purpose*

Mark & Billie Robinson

The Soul Purpose of Wealth Copyright © 2019 by IAW Titans Pty Ltd. All Rights Reserved.

All rights reserved. No part of this book may be reproduced in any form or by any electronic or mechanical means including information storage and retrieval systems, without permission in writing from the author. The only exception is by a reviewer, who may quote short excerpts in a review.

Cover designed by IAW Titans Pty Ltd

Mark & Billie Robinson
Visit our website at www.TheInternationalAcademyofWealth.com
Printed in Australia

First Printing: March 2019
IAW Titans Pty Ltd

ISBN-978-0-646-99947-0

CONTENTS

Introduction – Why this book and why now?..1
Part One – The banks have educated us to right where they want us to be..............13
    The world is drowning in debt and it's taking you with it..14
    Household debt in Australia..21
    The Wealth Quadrant...32
    Getting out of debt...39
Part Two – Building your Financial Independence Formula..52
    The financial independence formula...68
    Foundations of wealth..72
    The Future of Investing..98
    Adding another income stream...109
Part Three – The Ultimate Wealth Plan and putting it all together..........................112
    What it takes to be wealthy...116
    Putting it all together – the Ultimate Wealth Acceleration Plan..........................119
    Next steps...134

WARNING: NONE OF THIS IS ADVICE, NOT EVEN GENERAL ADVICE. THIS IS PURELY MY OPINION AND, AS FAR AS I'M AWARE, I AM STILL ALLOWED AN OPINION IN THIS COUNTRY. THIS IS FOR EDUCATIONAL PURPOSES ONLY AND IS BASED ON YEARS OF RESEARCH I HAVE PERSONALLY UNDERTAKEN. YOU COULD FIND THIS INFORMATION YOURSELF IF YOU STOPPED WATCHING NETFLIX OR GOT OFF FACEBOOK AND TINDER. YOUR PERSONAL CIRCUMSTANCES HAVE NOT BEEN CONSIDERED AT ALL.

If you would like advice specific to your personal circumstances, we urge you to talk to a financial professional who has achieved the results you are looking to achieve.

We also urge you to always do your own research (DYOR) and due diligence (DD). Never blindly take action on what we, or anyone, says or reports. It has never been more important to get yourself educated on the types of investments available. DYOR to find specific investments that will suit you. Take control of your future, your money, your choices. You will make smarter, more educated and ultimately more profitable decisions with your investing.

*PAST PERFORMANCE DOES NOT GUARANTEE FUTURE RESULTS. BUT YOU ALREADY KNEW THAT.

Testimonials

"A compelling, authentic and easy-to-read book offering real life, logical solutions that you want to and can apply immediately to effect positive change."
–Jane Voskamp Thomsen, text-based artist, and Paul Thomsen, business manager, New Zealand

"A must-read book if you really want to change and live the life you want. Easy to read and incredibly practical with exercises that get you to think about what you want and have clarity in creating, planning and tracking your Wealth Plan."
–Sim Chan, founder of Smarter Investment Management

"Mate, this is bloody good. It reads like I am sitting in the room listening to you – straight up, informative, blunt and actionable. It covers a lot of detail, but detail that can refloat your finances and stop you from sinking."
–Jeff Don, social worker and member of the International Academy of Wealth

"Mark's new book is written in a straightforward, easy to understand language. His action plan and steps to financial freedom are laid out step by step. I'll be taking much of what I've learned and applying it to my life from now on, so that I can be financially independent."
– Naomi Levin, CEO at Kuini Designs & Decor

"Mark and Billie have put together a body of work in this book, of which they should be very rightly proud! Within its pages you will find some things that will scare the pants off you but, more importantly, a guide to identifying where you are and a roadmap to get to where you want to go. I commend it to you as a great resource."
– Greg Watson, Home & Investor Finance Specialist at The Investor Hub

"Big day – our son has implemented his first investment, thanks to your education. Feels awesome seeing our 20-year-old starting his wealth journey. We wouldn't be here without you, Billie and the International Academy of Wealth community."
– Chris and Trudy Hartup, members of the International Academy of Wealth

Foreword by Randy Tate – Knowledge is power

I have spent the better part of three decades working to educate people around areas that I felt they were misinformed about, or just didn't know what was really going on. This includes teaching Grade 8s [Year 8s in Australia] about the importance of proper nutrition and the dangers of drug abuse, all the way to coaching CEOs of multi-million-dollar companies on the art of language and leadership. As the CEO of a global software company that is changing the very fabric of the financial services industry, I know that education of the masses around what is really going on with their wealth couldn't come at a better time. When Mark Robinson asked me to write the foreword to this book, *The Soul Purpose of Wealth*, I was happy and honored. This book hits at the heart of the problem – not just what's on the surface but everything underneath, from the individuals of the world to big governments. So, pay attention, as you just might discover the soul purpose of **your** wealth and, more importantly, what you can do about it.

I have known Mark Robinson for nearly 10 years. I met him on my first trip to Australia where I was – you guessed it – teaching at a seminar on creating wealth and running a business. If Mark takes on something, he only knows one speed and that is full throttle (if you don't believe me, ask his wife and kids). Over the last several years, as Mark and his wife Billie have built the International Academy of Wealth, I have had the pleasure of attending and speaking at several of their events which are eye-opening for all, whether you are a sophisticated investor or just starting out on your wealth journey. I also couldn't be more thrilled that he is putting the system the Academy team teaches into this book.

The financial services industry is ripe for disruption and the traditional way people have always invested – be it your superannuation fund in Australia or your 401k in the United States – is not designed to make you wealthy. As you go through the learnings in this book, pay special attention to the word 'compounding' as one of the anchors. Licensed professionals and governments do not explain to you that it is a two-way street, your losses can compound as well. Chew on this: if you have a traditional stock market investment – be it in the USA, Australia, London, Toronto, in a mutual fund or just a single share of Facebook – and you lose 50%, it takes from that point a gain of 100% to get you back to 0. Scary.

As you read this book, I have one simple request to help you get the most out of it: don't be right! Whatever you know (or think you know) may get turned a bit upside down in this read, and when this happens, instead of thinking to yourself (yes, thinking is involved here), "That's not correct," or "That's not how I would do it," change that thought to "Hmm, that's interesting. I better keep reading to understand it," or, better yet, send him an email and ask him to explain. If you can approach this book from that perspective and are willing to actively follow the guidance within, then you, my friend, are on your way!

I also want you to take notice of the title and that it has the word "soul" not "sole" in it. That's not a typo. As you read through this and find yourself excited about what may lie ahead or shocked about some of the debt numbers of governments, remember the word. I believe that happiness is our birthright and it is not solely tied to money. As you go through life making 'wealth' decisions, remember to ask yourself, "For the sake of what would I do that?" Your knee-jerk reaction is probably to say, "for the money," but that is almost never the answer.

One last little nugget for you pay close attention to as you read this book. Take note of the difference between financial freedom and financial independence and if one is better than the other. This will also help you answer the question from above "for the sake of what..." and as a matter of fact start right now, before you begin reading write it down. Put it here in the book.

I am reading this book for the sake of _____
_____
_____
_____
_____
_____

And I expect to learn _____
_____
_____
_____
_____

Now, enjoy the read. Mark writes just like he talks, straight and to the point. There is no BS here. The knowledge you are going to receive will empower you not only to identify the soul purpose of your wealth but how you can go and get it! Cheers!

– Randy Tate, CEO, iFlip Invest

Randy is a consumer software expert with a passion for entrepreneurs and growing companies. He has been an educational advocate for small business communities all over the world and has personally consulted and trained companies in countries including Australia, Europe, South Africa and others. As a former VP at Infusionsoft, Randy helped grow the company from $60 million in revenue to over $100 million, and prior to that was the president of executive coaching company Growth Choice. Randy has also led companies from the ground up. As CEO/co-founder of sporting goods distributor Game Day Athletics, he took the company from startup to acquisition by publicly traded industry giant Sport Chalet within four years. As CEO of iFlip Investor Inc, Randy has many responsibilities across the organisation, including oversight of all sales and marketing, customer experience and training, and the company's partner program. His leading cross-functional teams is allowing the company to grow at a record pace without compromising customer experience.

INTRODUCTION – WHY THIS BOOK AND WHY NOW?

For over 26 years, we have been part of the financial services industry. We have gone from working for a top four financial institution to running our own multi-company financial services business which includes mortgage broking, financial planning, property investing, accounting and insurance. We have seen the industry deteriorate before our eyes. Society's trust in financial services, and those that are a part of it, is at an all-time low. A recent survey we did within our own database cemented this. Every single person who replied to the survey stated they did not trust banks, superannuation companies and other investment "gurus".

Then we have the politicians who are more worried about their perks and votes than doing what is right for their country. This is not a problem isolated just to Australia. It feels as if we have been sold off to the highest bidder time and time again, and our politicians do not appear to be doing anything to stop it. It must stop or the once-dubbed "lucky" country will be virtually unliveable. Sad, yet true. Not many people we speak to have trust in our governments, no matter who is in power. That trust has gone a long time ago, but most people don't do anything about it as they have their own problems to worry about – like paying their rent or mortgage, school fees, power, phone, or Netflix. The list of expenses goes on and on. A major expense for over 65% of Australians is interest on their debt.

If the system that teaches us to build wealth is working, then why has the number of people who retire financially free not changed in 35 years? It is are unlikely to soon, either. It is even worse than people think or are being told. Governments are failing at balancing the books and are now in debt more than any other time in history. The Australian government owes approximately $714 billion and climbing every single day. The power of compounding works both ways (more on this throughout the book), debts as well as profits. America, the land of the free, owes over $61 trillion and has another $120 trillion in unfunded commitments such as the Patient Protection and Affordable Care Act (PPACA, also known as "Obamacare") and social welfare. Great Britain, Germany and France are all under the pressure of too much debt. This is not just a problem in the West either, with Japan and China owing trillions of dollars. The question I have is, "Who does the world owe all this money to?" The answer is a book in itself.

If we then bring the debt problem down to the people, we are owing more and more money every single day. Credit card debt, car loans, personal loans and mortgages are not enough for the ever-hungry debt machine. There is now Afterpay, Zip Pay and many others as well – payment options aimed at younger generations who want everything now. These services are being given out easily and frequently to our younger generation, and they are getting themselves into financial difficulty far too quickly. The banks and financial institutions have us right where they educated us, and it's time for us to make a stand and take control of our lives. Let's just say that again, **"The banks and financial institutions have us right where they educated us."** You get that, right?

Throughout this book, we share how you can get out of debt, and build multiple streams of income – no matter where you are starting from. It is not the amount of money you earn that determines whether you become financially independent. We know people who make over $400k per year and live pay cheque to pay cheque. It is, however, what you do with the money you earn that counts.

We know what it is like to build wealth and have the freedom to do what we want, when we want – only to have it all taken away from us. Starting again is easier when you have the tools and steps we share in this book.

Here are our definitions of 'Financial Freedom' and 'Financial Independence':

"Financial Freedom is where you have reached the point of having enough passive income to do what you want, but you don't quite understand how you got there. Financial Independence is when you know exactly how you got there and, if need be, you could get there again.

Financial Freedom can be given, won, or inherited, however Financial Independence is driven intentionally. It must be created, and crafted through knowledge, wisdom and continued education.

Therefore, one must travel the path of education to truly become financially independent."

We are giving you the formula you need to be financially independent within these pages – however, reading this book will not make you wealthy. You will need to act. Our "soul" purpose is to help you break the chains that are holding you back so that your soul can live a life on purpose. By sharing this information with as many people as we can, it will help to achieve **our** soul purpose.

When you finish reading this, you will need to decide. No matter what that decision ends up being, it will be the right one for you. Why? Because you made it yourself and you made it after reading this book, with more information about what's really going on than you had before.

We never have, nor will we ever, hold back the punches. We like to tell people straight, whether they are ready to hear it or not. So, if you are looking for a loving, caring, "she'll be right, mate" book, then this is not for you. If, on the other hand, you are open to hearing the truth, no matter how much it will hurt, then this book **is** for you. There is a reason why you have picked up this book to read. We are guessing it is because you are sick of hearing, and seeing, the BS being spruiked out there by everyone. We know we are. It is why we have a no-fluff filter inbuilt and, whether we're on stage, a guest on someone's podcast, or writing a post on Facebook, we say what is on our minds.

Enjoy the truth within these pages as it can set you, and your soul, free – if you are just a little bit curious.

We have broken this book into three parts:
- **Part One** speaks briefly about how we (the world and everyday people) got into this amount of debt. We have kept this as brief as possible. We speak about what debt management is, how much debt society is in and what you can do to get out of debt management.
- **Part Two** is getting ready and starting your investing journey.

- **Part Three** is the complete, step-by-step Ultimate Wealth Acceleration Plan.

All three parts can be started at the same time. You do not have to wait to be fully out of debt, nor do you need to have your financial house in order. All three parts work together and as one. Having said that, you may want to get a good grasp on each part first before putting the next step in place. We have included suggested steps, further reading, guides and other helpful links at the end of each part. You will also find space for notes, comments and answers to questions we ask. This allows you to keep this all in one place.

Remember, you do not have to travel this journey alone. This book gives you everything you need to become financially independent by yourself, a DIY (do it yourself) solution. Or you can tap into resources we have to speed up the process (done with you). Lastly, we have options that are as close to done for you as possible, to truly accelerate your financial independence. We have a saying, "*Those that seek advice, seek to blame others. Those that seek education, seek responsibility for their own decisions.*"

Therefore, we do not give advice. This book provides a road map of suggestions that we know, when applied correctly, will help you accelerate your education to allow you to be financially independent.

To your financial independence,

Mark & Billie

Our journey

We have spent over 26 years in the financial services industry and have worked with some major corporations here in Australia, and I am now officially an ex-financial planner. I handed my licence back in February 2018 so that I can freely share more education. Not having a licence allows us to speak what's on our minds and have an opinion that is 100% ours. We like that.

Look, we are not going to spend too long here or bore you with the details. We just want to share with you that, had we not done what we are telling you to do, we would have been broke and out of the game of wealth for three, four, even seven years.

14 years ago, we were so broke that at one stage we had to leave the groceries at the supermarket counter because we had no cash or credit left. Billie was pregnant with our second child at the time. Our business was just starting to take off. We look back and can see we weren't broke because of anything we had or hadn't done. We were broke because we were relying on one income stream to feed our family. While we believed in what we were doing, in our hearts and in our souls, we were cutting it very fine. It made us sweat, that's for sure! But the reality is that we made it through those times, things began to flow and the rest, as they say, is history. However, at the time, it felt like we were heading down a path that we had seen before.

Neither of us were born with a silver spoon in our mouths. We both come from hard-working families. What I learnt from my mum and dad was that they worked extremely long hours to earn their income. Their income was above average for the 1980s. It was what they did with it that counted.

I also learnt from them that true wealth has nothing to do with how hard you work or how much money you earn. It comes down to what you do with it and the strategy behind it.

Billie's parents were both pensioners for a significant part of their adult lives. Her father started his working life as a baker. He joined the army and worked various jobs when he returned home, before having to take a serviceman's pension due to what happened during his service. Her mother started out nursing, had children, and then worked in aged care. She later became a carer for her husband. They always did the best they could. Again, it wasn't about the money. It was about what they did with it and the strategy behind it that got them all through.

That time at the supermarket brought back these memories of our parents and we knew that we had to change because we were heading down the same path. Even though our business had hit a turning point, we were literally living pay cheque to pay cheque.

We spent hours and hours researching the wealthy and what they knew that we didn't. We were building our businesses but still relying mainly on me to produce the results. If I wasn't working, the family wasn't earning. What were the wealthy doing differently? What would it take for us to do what they were doing? We asked this every day for years.

During this time, we discovered that there was a simple formula to creating wealth. Fantastic!

And it goes like this: your active income (AI) plus your passive income (PI) plus your laptop income (LI) must be greater than your fixed expenses (FE) plus your investment expenses (IE) plus your lifestyle expenses (LE):

AI + PI + LTI > FE + IE + LE

We were falling into the trap set by the system, the banks and the big financial institutions. They had educated us to right where they wanted us! We were in the trap of living for the now. Our lifestyle expenses were bigger than our budget. The term 'champagne lifestyle on a beer budget' comes to mind. We were borrowing money to go on holidays, buying new cars, etc. All that did was increase our bad debt, which we would then convert into a personal loan and it would then become one of our fixed expenses. It was a soul-destroying cycle. This part we didn't learn from our parents. They had their mortgage but that was it. This 'debt management' lesson was all ours.

Once we discovered the formula, we acted straight away. We started to gradually build other streams of income outside our main businesses and pay down our consumer debt. Paying off our debt gave us more spare income to invest. This, in turn, built up our streams of income, which compounded over time. It has given us freedom, and a financial house built of bricks (more on that later).

In fact, our financial house has been strong enough to withstand an ex-employee personally costing us $1 million to fix his mistakes. About five years ago, we also invested a large chunk of cash into a strategy, only to see it disappear almost immediately. This last one destroyed a fair chunk of our wealth – and our minds, bodies and souls took a serious hit too.

If we didn't practise what we preach, we would have lost everything years ago. We have learnt over time that we not only need to have a strong foundation in our wealth, we also need a strong foundation within ourselves. The heart and soul of us needs to be strong and congruent with all that is going on in our lives. If they are not congruent, then we cannot believe there will be complete success. You would be surprised at just how much this holds you back from your life, and from an abundant life. The fact is money, wealth and abundance will flow effortlessly in your life once you truly believe it, in the absolute core of your being. It does take work and a bit of rewiring to think and feel differently.

It won't happen overnight, but it will happen... We've heard that before, right? It is true, though – it won't happen overnight, or in six months, or even 24 months. But it will happen if you are consistent with what you put in place. You must be an active participant, and if you are in a relationship then you both need to become active participants in your wealth creation. This simple yet effective formula has given our family an incredible life. It keeps getting better and better, even with the ups and downs we have had over the last five years.

What we are sharing works **if you apply the steps.** Taking actions from these lessons has allowed us an incredible lifestyle. We've been to China and Japan with a bunch of entrepreneurs; we've taken our kids around the world; we've been to Disneyland, New York, Rome Paris, Egypt. I'm not saying this to show off, guys. I just want to show you that if you take action from the contents of this book, and through the International Academy of

Wealth, you can also live like this.

Invitation

At the International Academy of Wealth, we believe in education and learning. We believe in the principles laid out in this book, and by no means do we think this is a conventional book. This book will help you to do something positive straight away to make changes in your financial situation. Some may think we are a little off-centre with our way of thinking, and that is OK. There may be a little controversy, and we know there may be some criticism. For some of our readers, there also may be a bit of personal discomfort as they consider their own financial house. And all of it is going to be OK. We truly believe, or at the very least hope, that you are reading this book because you want to make positive changes and find your soul purpose of wealth, to live your life on purpose. After you read this book, you will have a better understanding of what that all means.

The definitions of wealth, soul and purpose, as used throughout this book, are as follows:

Wealth, *noun*: a plentiful supply of a particular desirable thing.

Soul, *noun*: emotional or intellectual energy or intensity, especially as revealed in a work of art or an artistic performance.

Purpose, *noun*: a person's sense of resolve or determination.

By combining these together in the title of the book, we want to give you a true sense of what we have created here, within these pages. The "soul purpose" of wealth is to create an abundance of any desired thing that engages your soul with emotions and energy, and that will appeal to your sense of resolve and determination to make it happen.

It helps to have some material wealth in today's economy. When we speak to people about what wealth means, however, it's never about money. It's having an abundance of time, or abundance of health, freedom, travel, etc. Visualisations and manifestations work but only go so far. You still need to have a burning desire to achieve what you seek, to have the resolve and determination to get off the couch and take whatever action is required to become wealthy, to become your definition of wealth. You do not need a lot of money to be financially free. You can live in magical paradises on earth for less than $1,500 a month.

If you are open to understanding and determined to achieve, your definition of wealth is within your reach. If you are curious, you will find yourself exploring options that you may not have heard before.

We invite you to be part of this soul-driven purpose. As you read this book, please do the action steps and answer the questions. They are important and are designed to guide you in making changes. It will help you, we are sure of this.

We believe this book is one you can return to at most stages of your wealth creation journey.

We wish you well, and hope you enjoy this book.

What's your purpose?

Only you can work out what is your purpose in this life. Some people know it the minute they are born, while others find it late in their life. There is no right or wrong.

We love this quote from David Letterman: "*Everyone has a purpose in life. Perhaps yours is watching television.*" We love watching TV, mainly movies, and it is our go-to when we want to relax. We know our purpose in life is NOT to watch TV though. Our greatest purpose is to teach. When I was in my early teens, I had thoughts of being a policeman or a teacher. Billie was going to be a nurse. None of those happened and we are grateful they didn't. Teaching roles back then paid next to nothing (and still do, according to the teachers we speak to). We love sharing the knowledge we have collected over our years in the financial services industry. It has given us an incredible platform to share with anyone who is curious enough to listen to a different point of view.

Do you need to know your purpose to become financially independent? Nope. Does it help? Can do. What we do know is that being financially independent gives you greater freedom to find and see your purpose come to life, as opposed to being broke and living pay cheque to pay cheque.

In the spaces provided below, please write your answers to the two questions. Writing them down triggers parts of your brain and allows the information you are learning to be absorbed. This is why we have "biggest takeaway" sections throughout the book. You can also jot down any action points, facts that you may want to check for yourself, or even a note to pick up the dry-cleaning next week. This is your book. You decide how you use the pages within. We just hope it's not for lighting fires or steadying a wobbly table.

Why do you want to be financially independent?

_____
_____
_____
_____
_____
_____

Is it big enough for you to want to change your current habits? If yes, how so?

_____
_____
_____
_____
_____
_____

PART ONE – THE BANKS HAVE EDUCATED US TO RIGHT WHERE THEY WANT US TO BE

"The most important thing to do if you find yourself in a hole is to stop digging."
– Warren Buffett

THE WORLD IS DROWNING IN DEBT AND IT'S TAKING YOU WITH IT

The picture that's being painted is that everything is rosy, everything's on track and life is good. However, we do have to dig a lot deeper to find the truth, and this is where you must be open-minded. We believe our collective consciousness is starting to realise that not everything we're getting told is true or even real. When you dig deeper, you start to find out exactly what's going on in the world economy.

For example, Europe is close to imploding. We are going to give you some shocking stats.

Let's look at Greece, for example. A relatively small country, which owes $384 billion USD. Ireland owes $240 billion, and Spain now owes $1.4 trillion. Now, that's a lot of money for anybody, let alone a country that is not exactly a massive economic powerhouse.

So, here's an economic powerhouse – France. They owe $2.6 trillion. Italy, in our mind, is already bankrupt with 360 billion Euro (approximately $407 billion), and climbing, in bad loans. No country in Europe really wants to help bail them out. They've also just had their 2019 budget knocked back by the EU. Italy owes $2.8 trillion. Imagine how many pizzas you'd have to sell to get $2.8 trillion back!

The balance sheets of a lot of European banks are completely loaded with sovereign bonds (debt) from insolvent countries such as Italy, Greece, Portugal, Spain and Ireland. This is putting a lot of exposure and fragility on the European banking system. If the bond market suddenly decides to implode, European's major banks are going to be in massive trouble.

Even the largest and most powerful economy in Europe, Germany, owes $2.4 trillion.

Let's head over to Britain. They're pulling up stumps, they've voted to leave the EU and they are the second most powerful economy. They also owe $3.4 trillion. It's insane.

Coming a bit closer to our side of the world, Japan owes ¥1 quadrillion. If you ever wanted to know what comes after trillion, it's a quadrillion – just add three more zeroes. If we bring it back into USD, that's $9.6 trillion. Looking at that figure, it makes Greece look thrifty.

Where it gets worse is that the Japanese government is a top ten holder of 90% of the Nikkei 225 stocks. Further decline in their stock market threatens the government's very survival. Japan's debt is 229% of their GDP (Gross Domestic Product – a measure of the economic output of the country). The knockout punch for Japan will be triggered by the collapse of Europe. Europe is Japan's third largest trading partner and that's going to cause a domino effect. Europe will falter, then Japan, and that will lead to further economies getting smashed.

Most people don't realise that Japan's GDP is twice the size of the UK's, India's and France's and three times larger than Canada's, and that nine banks in Japan are in the top 100 largest in the world. To put that into perspective, the USA has 10. Japan is very much an integral part of the world economic system.

In the last financial crisis, Australia was saved by China's massive appetite for commodities. China has a bigger credit bubble than the United States does (we will chat about the USA soon). China's debt is $5.1 trillion – however, this figure now excludes local government financing vehicles (and we're not talking cars). We suggest you multiply this figure by at least 3.25. They are well over $18 trillion in debt. Then consider adding a figure for the Chinese population who are shadow banking outside of formal banks. In short, they owe a metric F$%^ton.

The real $600 billion ticking time bomb is that people don't realise that Chinese stocks have been absolutely hammered by more than 30% in the recent stock market decline. Their economy is slowing, and their debts are rising. You've got the trade war with President Trump, and it's really starting to push things to a breaking point. Shortly, companies and investors will be forced to sell their shares. It will be the final straw. Let us explain further.

In China, hundreds of companies have used their shares as collateral for borrowings. According to Bloomberg, $600 billion worth of shares have been put up by companies, founders and other major investors as collateral for loans. That's crazy! This equates to 11% of the country's stock market capitalisation.

When the share price falls, they are forced to sell their shares to maintain a certain debt to equity ratio. If it keeps declining, those shares are going to have to be sold as well. Suddenly, it's going to be a vicious cycle where if it keeps dropping, they've got to sell more shares, which means that the value will keep dropping, which means they've got to sell more shares. It's a financial disaster waiting to happen.

The USA is worse off than anyone else. At time of writing (early 2019), the US national debt was $21 trillion. The real concern is their future obligations. If we include these, you're looking at $164 trillion. That is massive, absolutely massive. That includes their social security and their Obamacare obligations.

Other concerns are:
- the percentage of Americans on disability benefits has tripled since 1970;
- and the number of children on disability benefits has increased by 1600%, which is sad.

Wall Street is the best at creating financial products that make them money and you, the end consumer, broke. They like to sell so-called corporate bonds (or junk bonds, as we like to call them) to unsuspecting, financially uneducated people. Junk bonds are what happens when companies (public or private companies) borrow from the public, as opposed to going through banks. The returns are higher than bank interest rates.

The oil sector borrowed $14 trillion a few years back, which is now due to be paid back or refinanced. This was back when oil was between $85 and $120 per barrel. In the last couple of years, it's been nowhere near that. This is putting a strain on a lot of oil companies who borrowed some of this $14 trillion. If only 10% of these loans default, it's going to be five times bigger than the 2008 financial crisis. The real concern for us is that a lot of our superannuation funds (or what Americans call a 401k) are invested in these so-called junk bonds. We don't want to blame the superannuation funds, because it's not really their fault. Wall Street wraps them up into these packages and rates them AAA – "safe" investments.

We just want to end with this – the world itself owes over $73 trillion, and we want you to ask this: who to? Seriously, who does the world owe $73 trillion dollars to? Who had $73 trillion to lend in the first place? Let's hope it's to us!

Don't get us started on this – we're not going to go down that rabbit hole here. We just want you to really think about that because, at the end of the day, there's something funny going on and it has been for decades.

Why should you care? Think about this: China, Japan and the United States are the top three largest trading partners for Australia. If something happens to them, 47.2% of our exports would be in jeopardy when those economies falter.

Debt has gone from the luxury of a few, to the convenience of the many, to an addiction for most, to a disease for all. It is a virus that has spread to every aspect of our economy. There is a cure for this virus, and it is contained within these pages.

P.S. We love how Fiscal Cliff (via 9GAG) explains it in two simple lessons:

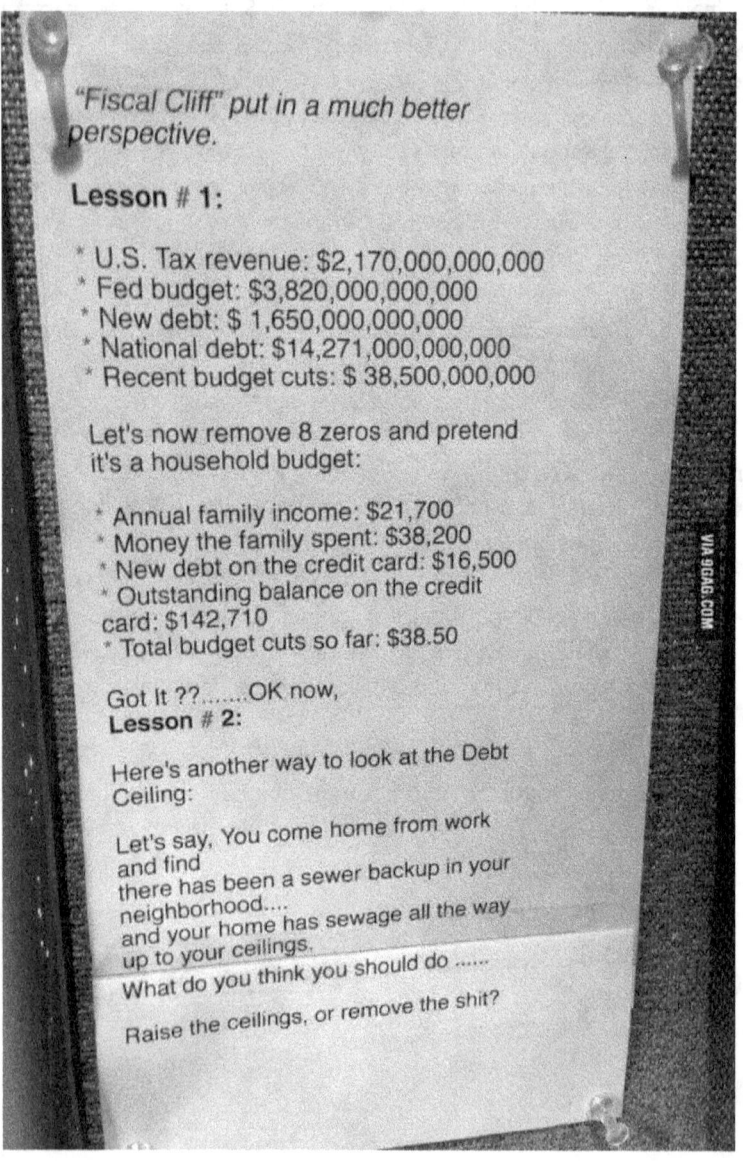

Don't be a statistic – it's killing you

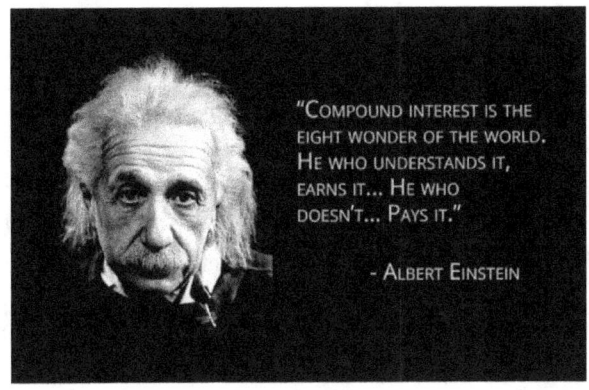

Albert Einstein said, "*Compound interest is the eighth wonder of the world. He who understands it earns it, he who doesn't pays it.*"

We will share more on this later in the book, with clear examples of both.

Below is a Facebook post I did on December 14, 2018, which clearly shows that most people do not understand compounding interest. They are being led into more and more debt, which allows us to be controlled for life (unless we do something about it).

"December is a BIG month for car sales. September this year, Australia borrowed $1.19 billion to buy cars. So, Australia will borrow more than that in December based on previous stats. This means that Australians will need to find over $40 million extra in January to pay for their cars.

Australia either increased or approved $1.5 billion in credit card limits in September. Again, this will be more in December. This plus the car loans.

Come January, they will need to find $29 million to cover the interest payments.

JUST F$#%^ng STOP IT!

The lenders are the best educators, marketers and manipulators out there. They give away finance such as credit cards and cars loans like crack dealers hand out the first hit. They know that once you owe, 95% of you will owe for life.

A $38k credit card paying the min repayment will take you 141 years to pay off and over $283k in interest and charges.

There is a better way to get out of debt and start to be in control of your decisions.

Look at your spending habits and your income and expenses. If most of your income goes to paying lenders, it's time you woke up and made changes.

The above stats are just one month's worth, which is bloody scary. To me, the stats prove that most people do not understand compounding interest and are setting themselves up to be in debt and controlled for most, if not for all, of their adult life."

This post was shared and commented on by a lot of people. Here is hoping it got through to some of them.

We were at a school assembly for our eldest child's senior secondary school program. The students are there to decide what subjects they should be looking at in the lead-up to their final year. We were having an enjoyable evening until the principal of the school started speaking about university and student loans, and how it would make your uni life "easier" if you borrow to get through. F%^$! Say what?

If we hadn't promised our kids when they were younger that we would not speak up at their school on topics we felt strongly about, the you-know-what would have hit the fan. Look, we don't blame the principal. She thought she was doing the right thing because she has been educated and conditioned into thinking that way. What no one understands is that student debt is payable for life. If you need to claim bankruptcy later in life, a student debt is still payable. You cannot wipe out a student debt by going bankrupt.

Australian household debt has steadily risen over the past three decades as more of us aim to own homes and continue to rely on products such as car loans and credit cards to fund our lifestyles. The ratio of household debt to income has more than doubled between 1995 and 2015, going from 104% to 212% (according to the Organisation for Economic Co-operation and Development data released in 2015). For example, if the average person earns $80,000 net, they owe $169,600.

While many other developed countries have seen a decline or "levelling out" of personal debt since the 2008 global financial crisis, Australia's debt levels have continued to increase. As a result, Australia is now reported to have some of the highest personal debt levels in the world.

Global comparisons of household debt usually look at the total owed as a percentage of net income. Australians rank fourth highest in the world next to Denmark, the Netherlands and Norway.

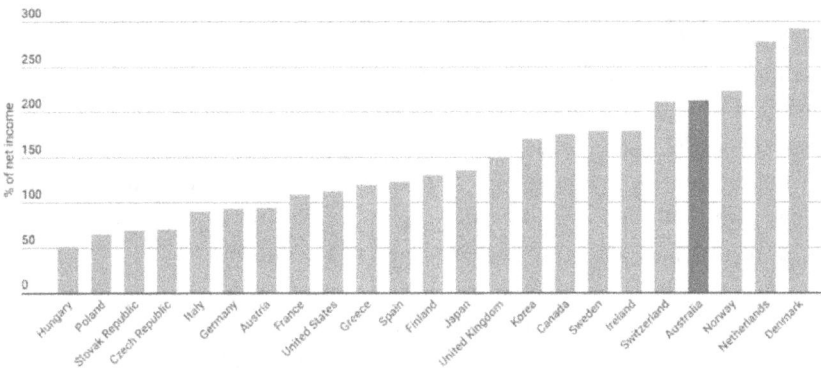

HOUSEHOLD DEBT IN AUSTRALIA

Debt is a reality for most Australians. Over recent years, rising property prices, declining interest rates and easier access to consumer credit has seen Australian households grow more comfortable with debt. However, high levels of debt, when considered against the value of current household income and assets, indicate vulnerability in the event of an economic shock – such as increases to interest rates, the loss of a job, illness or injury, a change in family circumstances or a drop in asset prices.

This section examines the debt level and profile of Australian households using two measures based on definitions used by the Organization for Economic Co-operation and Development (OECD):

- debt-to-income ratio, where over-indebted households had debt three or more times their annual disposable income;
- and debt-to-asset ratio, where over-indebted households had debt equal to 75% or more of the value of assets.

Household debt is on the rise

Over the past 12 years, the proportion of households holding debt has remained almost unchanged – 73% in 2003-04, compared to 74% in 2015-16. However, the average household debt (after adjusting for inflation) has almost doubled, increasing from $94,100 in 2003-04 to $168,600 in 2015-16. This increase was mostly driven by property debt, which has increased steadily over the years – from $78,400 in 2003-04 to $149,600 in 2015-16, and it is now expected to top $200,000 in 2019.

With recent hikes in some of Australia's key property markets (Sydney and Melbourne, amongst others) and ready availability of credit, property prices and household debt have risen hand in glove.

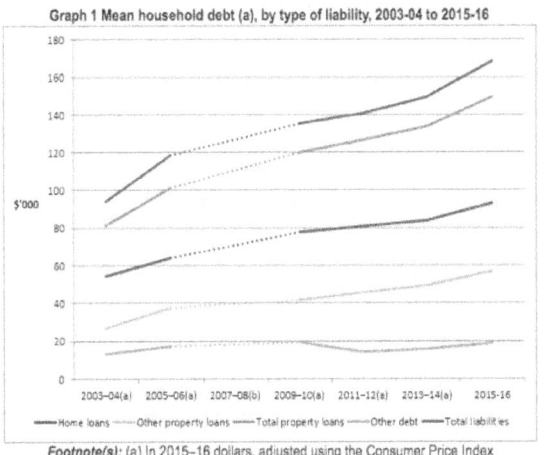

Graph 1 Mean household debt (a), by type of liability, 2003-04 to 2015-16

Footnote(s): (a) In 2015-16 dollars, adjusted using the Consumer Price Index
(b) Comprehensive wealth data was not collected in 2007-08
Source(s): ABS Survey of Income and Housing

In 2015-16, based on the ratio of debt to either income or assets, around 3 in 10 households (29%) were classified as 'over-indebted'. Remembering that the definition of 'over-indebted' is defined as more than 3x household income or more than 75% of household assets, the following are interesting statistics from the Australian Bureau of Statistics (ABS):

- Owners with a mortgage were the most likely households to be over-indebted (47%).
- Households with a reference person aged between 25-34 years (33%) and 35-44 years (34%) are among those most likely to be over-indebted based on age group.
- High income households were more likely to be over-indebted.
- Sydney and Melbourne had the highest number of over-indebted household at 407,000 and 419,600 households, respectively.
- Over-indebted households were over twice as likely as other indebted households to have a home loan (76% of over-indebted households, compared to 34% of other indebted).
- Most over-indebted households (77%) lacked sufficient "liquid" assets to cover a quarter of the value of their debts.

Whilst the property market has grown, the bank's share of that growth has also increased, and a large proportion of Australia's middle-income-earning population is shackled with an overburden of debt.

In terms of the demographics of least indebted households, there are no real surprises from the analysis: households with a person aged 65 or older (5%), households that owned their home out-right (4%) or rented (9%), and households whose main source of income was from government pensions and allowances (7%) were least likely to be over-indebted.

These are the people that the banks are unable to lend large chunks of money to, reflecting consumer protection laws. Those that the banks can lend lots of money to... well, they do. Some people are protected, but they are burdened in different ways.

While the most important factor driving over-indebtedness, statistically speaking, is mortgage lending, the continuing ready-availability of consumer credit – through credit cards and personal loans – is a phenomenon that affects ALL household groups. Both high-income earners and the unemployed are accumulating high levels of credit card debt.

One in five Australians (20%) who are earning between $101,000 and $150,000 per annum now own three or more credit cards and hold an average of $5,978 in credit card debt, according to a finder (https://www.finder.com.au/) survey of 2,085 Australians. The survey revealed that the average credit card debt is $4,268, with the level of debt accrued generally rising with income. We call people in this category THE PRETENDER (more on that later).

However, the data found that respondents with no income also hold a similar level of debt — $3,774 in credit card debt on average. People in this category are called THE SPENDER (again, more on that later). According to finder, this group owes more than those earning between $50,000 and $75,000 ($3,459), with 17% also stating that they have more than one credit card.

Australians earning up to $25,000 owed an average of $3,802, with nearly a fifth (18%) having multiple cards. Additionally, respondents earning between $26,000 and $50,000 owe $3,761 of debt, while a quarter have more than one credit card.

Further, according to finder's State of the Credit Card Market report 2018, Australians made more purchases using their credit cards in 2017 than 2016, rising from $2.5 billion to $2.7 billion. In 2017, Australians spent an average of $1,573 per month on their credit cards.

Overall, there are just under 16.7 million credit cards in Australia, with an additional 8,298 Australians issued with credit cards in 2017, according to Nest Egg (https://www.nestegg.com.au), a news source about planning, investing and managing your retirement.

Do you really want me to go on? How's the soul feeling right now? But don't worry. Keep reading. There is a way to ensure you become financially independent and find your soul purpose of wealth to live your life on purpose.

Community experts case study – Pete & Dierdre

Here's an example of a client of ours getting back in control of their debt after a bump in the road, with help from Investor Hub founder Greg Watson.

Peter and Dierdre both had well-paying jobs – she was in insurance and he was a corporate consultant. They had a home in Sydney and a young son. But, as things sometimes happen, Peter and Dierdre had a falling out and they separated. They were apart for about a year and when they came to see us, they had just reconciled. However, things weren't the same, economically speaking.

What had happened was water under the bridge. But the result of 12 months apart, and essentially running two households in one of the most expensive cities in the world, was that they had both lived beyond their means. They spent more than they earned, their credit cards were all maxed out, Peter had bought a new car on credit and, overall, they'd racked up about an extra $100,000 in debt. This was smothering them both financially and emotionally as they picked up the pieces and re-embarked on their life together.

Thankfully, they had built up equity in their family home and we were able to tap into that asset to give them some relief from the tide of personal debt lapping at their chins.

The result? By consolidating their debts, we decreased their outgoings by over $4,000 per month. $4,000 a month! No wonder it was stifling them! Peter said: "Greg, thanks so much for helping us out. After sorting all this out, we've got our life back again!"

Following our advice, Peter & Dierdre accelerated their repayments to reduce the debt burden so that they weren't paying off credit card debt over 30 years, and they were able to recover from that bump in the road.

What can a mortgage advisor do for you? – Greg Watson

Greg Watson is not your average mortgage advisor. With an extensive academic background including a Master's degree in Economics and a Diploma in Financial Services; and prior professional background as an economic and banking analyst, CFO of an Australian mutual bank, financial consultant and small business owner; Greg brings a wealth of knowledge and information to the table to combine with extensive practical experience in the mortgage business.

Almost 60% of mortgage loans funded in Australia are now written through mortgage advisors, or brokers. That is testament to the professionalism and quality of our profession and recognising the value that a professional brings to the table, to your advantage.

There are a number of reasons why you should use a mortgage advisor, and there are specific advantages that The Investor Hub brings to the table.

We value integrity – it's our #1 core value. We value transparency in both the conduct of our team and the solutions we provide, and *Our Promise* to our clients is that you can always rely on us for that.

Having a highly qualified professional team with decades of experience should give you confidence that you are dealing with someone who knows what it takes to help you achieve your financial goals and aspirations, whether that be buying a home or investment property, refinancing, debt consolidation or gearing up to invest outside property. We have a depth of experience in all facets of finance.

It pays to have the best advice from the start. We know that our service adds value to you as a home owner or investor – to save you money, and to make you money. You get that from a professionally qualified mortgage advisor – and you'll get that from us at The Investor Hub.

Three ways to control us

Three ways to control us are via mind, matter and money. Originally, we were going to go into a bunch of history and speak about how they used to control us in the early days via a feudal society with kings and queens owning everything before turning to slavery down to how they now control us financially. However, we feel that it all ties in with controlling our minds, matter and money.

Mind

The mainstream media does its best to control our mind, our thoughts, and therefore our actions — via advertising, news and TV programs (it's called programming for a reason, it's programming your mind!), and censorship.

Years ago, we ended up buying two new cars. It seemed so out of the blue both times. You see, we love watching the cricket, especially the Boxing Day test match. It's our thing. That particular year, they were heavily advertising a Ford Territory. In mid-January, I surprised Billie with one. It was the family's first new car and, don't get me wrong, we loved it. Great car. Looking back, though, we didn't really go looking at any others. The following year, I bought Billie her first new car — a Holden Cruze. Guess which car they advertised during the cricket that year? Yep, the Holden Cruze! Plus, we may or may not have bought some KFC over those summers as well.

Nowadays, we are more aware and we control our thoughts, not the TV. But not everyone is as aware, and the advertising companies, marketers, financial institutions and governments know that. 95% of the population can be controlled by simply putting their agenda in front of them enough times that they believe that what they see is either true or what they need.

Matter

In matter and the physical, we are controlled less directly these days. Yet, if you think about it, they definitely control or want to control us physically. Think about the types of food they allow to be advertised as healthy, and the number of medical drugs that are out there. Australia and the USA have nearly 75% of men and 60% of women classed as overweight. It's much easier to control unhealthy people than healthy ones.

Money

This is by far the easiest way to control people these days. If you combine it with their mind and their matter (physical), then most lose all hope and must rely on the system (government and banking) to survive. This is why banks advertise credit cards, personal loans and mortgages as much as they do. They know, like a crack dealer, that once they have you hooked, there is no going back. You think that the only way to live is to borrow more money to keep up with the lifestyle the advertisements promised.

Start to take full control over your mind, matter and money, or you will be stuck in the system forever. The financial system has been designed to control you from birth to death. Most of us learn our money control via our parents, who got it from their parents, and so on. They know that there is a good chance you will also pass it on to your kids. They, in turn, will pass it on to theirs. In the next chapter, I'll briefly share how the banking system works.[1]

---

[1] To understand the history of money read or watch 'The Ascent of Money' by Niall Ferguson.

The financial matrix

The more complex the system seems, the less people will want to understand it, and therefore the less people will understand how the system controls them. We believe this is one of the main reasons why people have lost their trust in the system — in banks, superannuation funds, companies, etc. You cannot blame them, either. However, now that you are reading this book, at least you can decide if you want to ignore this information or use it to build a life free of stress and worrying about where the money will come for the next unexpected expense. Without worrying about debt, and when you have enough income to work less, life's choices open up. Your choices become, well, *your* choices.

We have tried to simplify the financial system as much as we can in the diagram below. If you understand that the global banking system has control of nearly every single country in the world, most companies and over 95% of the employed population in one shape or form, then you have a handle of how it works.

The bottom line is:
- We owe money to the banking system.
- Companies owe money to the banking system.
- The government owes money to the banking system.
- The government continues to increase or create new taxes to cover ever-increasing shortfalls in their budget. These shortfalls are created by incompetent politicians who should be held accountable.
- Companies must increase prices to pay for these taxes.
- Companies owe $20 trillion to banks in America alone, putting pressure on their bottom line.
- We must pay higher prices to pay for the cost of living.
- If we do not have a spending plan in place, more than likely we will borrow to get by, increasing our debt.
- For most, our net investable income is shrinking.
- The banking system continues to employ the best of the best marketing strategies to ensure you continue to rack up the debt and stay chained to the system it has created.
- When it all turns to crap and no one can afford to pay anyone back, the people who own the banks don't care because they will then be able to buy all the

assets in the world for a fraction of the cost, increasing their wealth along the way.
- 95% of the working and middle class will have their wealth wiped out within the next five to ten years, tops — in our opinion.

Be part of the 5% that gets to not only keep but also increase their wealth.

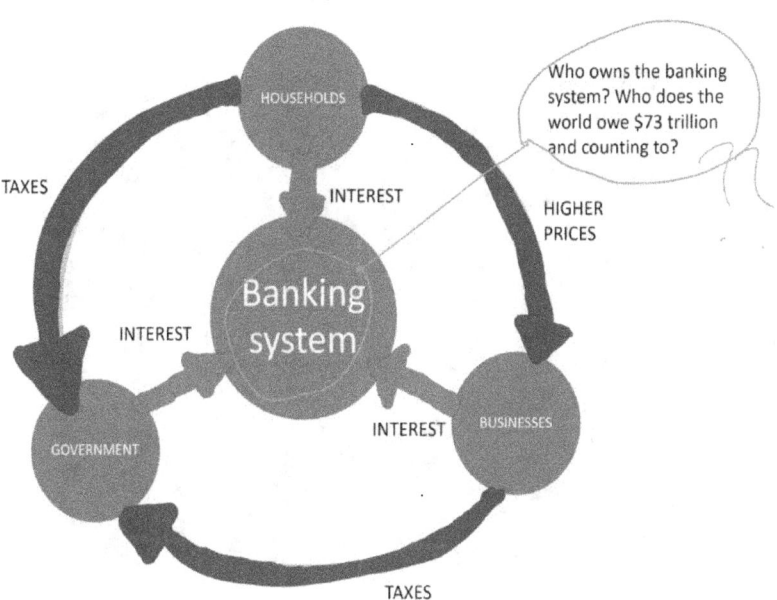

THE WEALTH QUADRANT

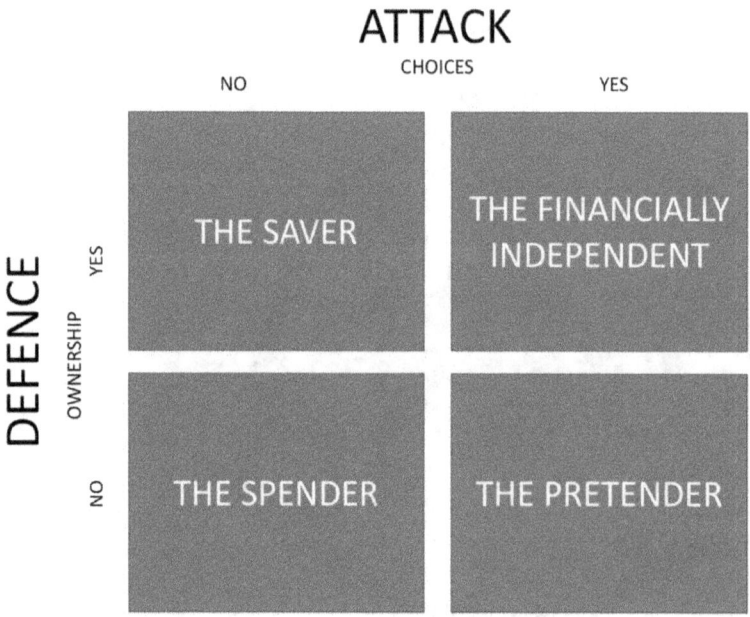

The Wealth Quadrant determines what financial type you are. There are four main types of people who are trying to build their wealth. These incorporate their defensive style, and their attack style. From their actions, it will determine the choices and the ownership they will have throughout their lives.

The idea of defence and attack in your wealth creation strategies is not new. We have spoken about this in one of our live education programs called "The Wealth Game". Creating wealth is just a game. It's easy when you know the rules, and easier again when you make the rules. However, the idea for the diagram came from Orrin Woodward. Orrin is a *New York Times* best-selling author with over 2 million books sold in eight languages. We have modified it to reflect how we see each quadrant.

To us, defence is more than reducing expenses. It covers things like insurances, and structures like companies, trusts and self-managed super funds. The same goes for attack. Attack is more than investing — it is investing wisely, knowing what you are investing in and why, having the right team around you, having the right strategy, and being in the right community.

Let's look at the types of people in the Wealth Quadrant.

THE SPENDER

The SPENDER is just that. They spend anything and everything. While they may have dreams, their goal is to win lotto and tell the boss to... well, you know what they want to say. They have no ownership, and very little control over what their life will look like. They have gone into debt for cars, holidays, parties, clothes, and nights out. They have an "I'll pay it tomorrow" attitude. They think that life is against them and can quite often come across as entitled. The world owes them something. It's always someone else's fault that they are broke.

The statistics in the western world are all very similar and show that 50% of people have zero net worth. Not one cent. When their debts are subtracted from their assets, nothing is left. In fact, most would show a negative balance — they owe more than they own. Years of hard work with nothing to show for it. The people in this quadrant have NO plan of defence or attack. They have no ownership of assets and very few choices. Most of these people believe there is no winning the game of wealth. They have no choice but to work harder and they hope that something will be there in retirement from the government, because they feel they are entitled to it. If you are in this quadrant, we have experts who can get you on the path to becoming financially independent.

THE PRETENDER

The second group in the bottom right-hand quadrant has debt and owns some assets. They tend to like the champagne lifestyle. They take nice holidays and drive the latest model car (all on borrowed money). They like to feel significant, like they have status. They look financially independent and they might even feel financially independent for a while, until the debt and, more importantly, the stress of managing the debt catches up with them. Every pay rise increases their false sense of significance. They tend to spend more than the actual pay rise they just received and head further into debt. While they have choices, paying for them via debt is a very dangerous game and can leave them vulnerable, should they be laid off or when the economy takes a turn for the worse. They are one pay day away from moving into the SPENDER quadrant.

To be fair, though, this quadrant is generally hard-working, intelligent and keen to learn. It's mainly due to the way the banks have educated us that they fall into this quadrant. We fell into this quadrant without the help of our parents. Like we said earlier, we own this lesson.

This quadrant also does not play good defence. They do not have a spending plan and they live beyond their means. They accumulate debt in order to look like they have choices, and to have freedom and the lifestyle. They borrow for cars and for a bigger and better house and to fund their vacations via debt. They might not have insurances in place for the 'what if' scenarios life can throw our way — such as divorce, sickness, death and redundancy. All the pay rises in the world can't keep them ahead of compound interest. At some point, it will catch up and consume their wages. This is why having a financial defence plan will prepare you for the risks of living.

Lastly, one of the biggest concerns of this group is that some of them are unteachable. Orrin states it best: "They know it all, show it all and owe it all, believing the ability to accrue debt makes them a financial wizard." If you are in this quadrant (Billie and I have been in here before), you have the best opportunity to become financially independent as you generally have some assets, good income and, if open to learning, great work ethics to speed up your wealth.

THE SAVER

Ah, the SAVER. These guys are, without a doubt, one of the more secure categories in the Wealth Quadrant. They know their defence plan. Yet that is all they play. Defence, defence, defence. They have ownership. They have their spending plan in place. They have the right insurances in place, and money tucked away for a rainy day. Yet they can only make choices that fit within their current reality. Without learning how to play the attack game and then applying the knowledge, defence is all they can do.

To win any game, you need to play defence and attack. Their idea of attack is getting a pay rise. When you factor in things like inflation and taxes, there is very little pay rise left — let alone enough to call it your attack plan. While their biggest strength is their financial discipline, it is also their biggest weakness. They tend to live the "I can't afford it" mentality. They live below their means by surrendering their dreams. They could still live for today and plan for tomorrow if they just played some attacking strategies. You have built the foundations exceptionally well, now it's time for attack!

At the International Academy of Wealth, we are unique in that we focus on defence as well as attack. We show you how to reduce your spending, reduce your debt and increase your income streams. This way, you can start to live the life of your dreams sooner. Learning to play defence *and* attack will allow you to achieve what you want, rather than just settling for the life you can afford now.

"You can't steal second [base] if you don't take your foot off first."
— *Mike Todd*

THE FINANCIALLY INDEPENDENT

The FINANCIALLY INDEPENDENT have both choices and ownership. Choices on what they want to do for the day, week, and month for the rest of their lives. They have ownership in foundational assets that will outlast their life time and beyond — such as property, blue chip shares, gold, silver, Bitcoin, etc. They have invested heavily in their personal development and in their wealth education. If you do not invest in yourself first, you will never make it to this quadrant. You do not have to go through each quadrant to get to financially independent — the journey isn't SPENDER → PRETENDER → SAVER → FINANCIALLY INDEPENDENT. You can take the steps required from any quadrant and head towards the financially independent quadrant. It is that simple. You have started to by buying and reading this book. But just doing that will not get you to this quadrant.

You need to:
- Play defence as well as attack;
- Take action;
- Live below your means;
- Start building other income streams;
- Understand the power of compounding;
- And follow the steps contained within these pages.

By using the power of compounding, the FINANCIALLY INDEPENDENT accelerate their choices and the ownership of their lives. This frees them from the constraints of money and time, so they can focus on their soul purpose. By decreasing your expenses and expanding your financial education, your debt will decrease and your income streams will increase. Compounding this process will lead you to financial independence. Everything you need to achieve this is within this book.

It is laid out for you, so you have the choice of:
- Doing nothing,
- Doing it yourself,
- Or having it done with you.

It's a simple choice, yet each one will have a massive impact on which quadrant you will live your life.

Remember, it is not how much a person makes that determines whether one is poor, but rather how much goes into investment versus expenses. So, what are expenses and what are investments? An expense is money spent with no expectation of a return, whereas an investment is money invested for an expected return. Make sure you invest your time and money wisely when moving forward.

This book is focussed on the money part of wealth. But there is so much more to wealth than just money. What we want to do, though, is get you thinking about what you would do with any extra money that you create. The next exercise will help you visualise what is possible.

Exercise – Money

We want you to imagine what an extra $100 a week in cash flow or income would do. What would you do with it? Would you go out on a date with your spouse or partner? Would you pay down some debt? Would you let that $100 a week compound over a set period? Write down your answers below. Take your time.

_____
_____
_____
_____
_____

Now imagine it's $250 a week. What would you do with that?

Now imagine it's $500. What could you do with $500 a week extra? Would you be financially independent and be able to quit your job if you wanted to?

Now imagine it's $2,000.

Imagine the figure that you need to become financially independent, where you could do whatever you want. What would you be doing? What would you do with it?

We get you to do this exercise because, at the end of the day, if we don't know what we would do with it, it's almost a case of what's the point of creating more wealth? We think of it this way — why would the Universe/Buddha/God (or whatever you believe in) give you more responsibility or more money if you can't even handle the responsibility or the money you have right now?

If you think of it from a job perspective, why would your boss give you more responsibility and then potentially a pay rise when you're not even looking after the responsibilities that you have right now? And it's the same in business. Why would customers give you more money if you're not fulfilling the promises that you have already given them? With finance and money, why would the Universe give you more money when you don't even have control of, and aren't being responsible with, the money that you have right now?

GETTING OUT OF DEBT

You do not have to be completely out of debt to start investing, but you do need to have an active debt management plan in place which you can monitor and review. Being stuck in the debt trap is the fastest way to kill your soul to the point of almost no return. The system, governments (although they are now trapped themselves) and banks know this and it is, perhaps, their goal to keep as many people in debt for as long as possible. **You can control your debt.** You just need to adjust a few things first.

Remember, a person cannot fix in mere months what it has taken years to stuff up. All real change must start with not only a change in thinking, but also consistent action. Debt is something we tend to avoid until it's too late. You will need to have the courage to go against the big marketing machines of the financial institutions and, closer to home, friends and family who say they want you to succeed, yet subconsciously distract you by keeping you on the same path as them.

> *"To live the life you always wanted, you are going to have to face the things you have been avoiding".*
> *–Orrin*

We love this saying from Orrin Woodward: "*Stop taking your own advice. If you are not happy with the results you are producing, perhaps it's time to stop taking your own advice.*"

As stated several times already — and we will continue to keep hounding you on it — to get out of debt, you will need to make changes to a number areas of your life. Warren Buffett, the world's most successful investor, says there are two keys to financial success:

- disciplined spending habits (minimised expenses),
- and careful investment strategies (maximised investments) to compound assets.

He also tells us, in his speech to the Nebraska Educational Forum[2] on October 11, 1999, to "*stay away from credit cards*" and "*Invest in yourself as much as you can. You are your own biggest asset by far.*" There is a good chance that you have "relaxed" spending habits, to put it nicely, and zero investment strategies — which is why you are in so much debt in the first place.

To get out of debt, you need to do the opposite of what the banks want you to do. They want you to pay the minimum amount per month off your debt. This compounds the interest (as they calculate it daily) and makes it close to impossible to pay off in two lifetimes, let alone just yours.

Check out these screenshots of a $38k credit card taking 141 years to pay off. We bet if you looked closely at your debts, you would find similar small print as well. The sooner you start, the sooner you change compound interest from working against you to working for you.

Opening balance at 21 Nov	$37,769.95
New transactions and charges	$1,264.17
Payments/refunds	-$761.00
Closing balance at 20 Dec	$38,273.12
Next statement period	21 Dec 2018 - 18 Jan 2019

Total amount owing	$38,273.12
Minimum payment	$765.00
Payment due by	14 Jan 2019

Your account is overlimit.
Please pay the overlimt amount of $273.12 immediately to ensure you can continue transacting on your account.

Minimum Repayment Warning: If you make only the minimum payment each month, you will pay more interest and it will take you longer to pay off your balance. For example:

If you make no additional charges using this card and each month you pay...	You will pay off the Closing Balance shown on this statement in about...	And you will end up paying estimated total interest charges of...
Only the minimum payment	141 years, 1 month	$292,825.74
$1,971.20	2 years	$9,035.78, a saving of $283,789.96

If you make only the minimum payment each month, you will pay more interest and it

You will pay off the Closing Balance shown on this statement in about...	And you will end up total interest charg
141 years, 1 month	$292,825.74
2 years	$9,035.78, a saving of

ents?
edit card repayments, please contact us on 1300 130 107. We may be able to assist ition, we use the cash advance rate and apply it to the entire balance.

For us, personally, we didn't have a long-term financial plan to guide our decision making. We didn't practice disciplined spending habits because our emotions consistently trumped our logic. This led to us having compound interest leveraged against us, rather than working for us. We realised that while we went to sleep at night, the compound interest didn't, and we were waking up more broke than the day before! We know how depressing and soul destroying this can be. But once a person eliminates debt, their money begins to accumulate quickly. It is a very freeing and soulful time.

Here are the steps we suggest you take to get out of the debt management system and start to become financially independent.

1. Start tracking your expenses. There are so many apps out there that can help you with this. The one we love is Monefly. Head over to their website or use this link http://www.monefly.com?afmc=The-4708. It is a free service and the team continue to make great improvements all the time. You must track your expenses somehow. It is the only way to capture all of them so you can determine which ones serve you and which ones don't. Do you really need Netflix, Stan, cable TV and movies on demand? Or do you think that maybe you could do without one or three of them for a while, so that you can create wealth? It's your choice.

2. Make a list of all your expenses and all your income. This is your starting point. We explain more about your starting point in Part Three.

3. Make a list of all your assets and liabilities. This is everything you own and everything you owe. Include any bills you are behind in as well. Again, this is part of your starting point. Subtract your expenses from your income. This will give you what we call your net investable income. For now, call it "Man, is that all I have left?" NOTE: the figure may be in the negative, i.e. you have more expenses than you have income. This is easy to fix if you truly want to change. See the tips section for more information.

The information in your answers to the above will determine which of the following steps you need to follow. Some may not be applicable and that's awesome — you are closer than you might think. If you have a positive number, then move to step 8. If not, then move to step 4.

4. So, your number is negative. You need to change this ASAP. Today, not tomorrow. List all the 'things' you have purchased that you no longer need or have never used. Be honest, otherwise these steps can't help you. Sell them for whatever you can and, for now, park the cash in a bank account that you cannot touch for a while. When you become financially independent, you may want to buy a similar item then. For now, if there's any losses from selling those items, then call it a wealth education expense. They say we pay for our education in one way or another. The more 'junk' you can offload, the better — especially from an energy perspective.

5. You need to increase your income, decrease your expenses, or both. It is that simple. Otherwise, you will continue to go backwards and compound the problem. **IF YOU DO NOT WANT TO DO WHATEVER IT TAKES TO GET YOUR "BOOKS" TO BALANCE WE CANNOT HELP YOU. YES, WE ARE YELLING DIRECTLY AT YOU!**

6. Decrease your expenses. Yep, you might have to forgo going out every weekend for a while. You might need to cook at home and not eat out or order in. That's OK.

7. If your negative balance is quite high or you have creditors constantly ringing you, please bring in an expert in debt negotiation. They know how to communicate with your creditors, banks, financial institutions etc.

8. Increase your income using some of the suggestions in the tips section.

Once you have completed these steps, start building your debt reduction plan. This screenshot is an example of our debt reduction calculator:

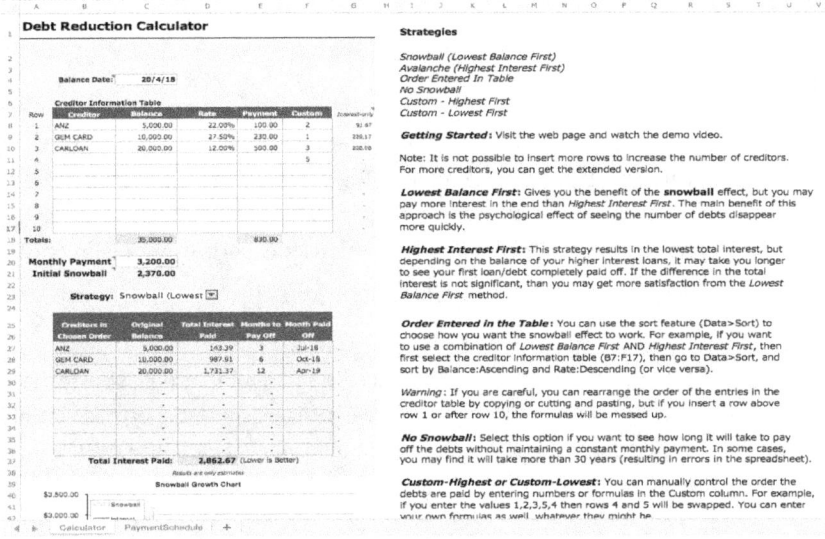

The calculator explains the different methods that you can look at to reduce your debts faster. Personally, whichever one you choose, paying the minimum amount off all your debts, bar one, is the fastest way to achieve your freedom from debt.

The best methods for debt reduction are:

Lowest balance first: Pay your lowest balance first. It gives you the benefit of the snowball effect. You may pay more interest in the end than paying off the highest first, however the main benefit is the psychological effect of a quick reduction in the number of debts. Once you pay off your first debt, you move onto the next, and so on and so on.

Highest interest first: Lowest total interest but, depending on the balance of your higher interest loans, it may take longer to see your first loan/debt completely paid off. If the difference in the total interest is not significant, then you may get more satisfaction from paying off the lowest balance first.

Tips

- Be honest with your situation. No one can help you if you won't help yourself. There may be underlying reasons why you keep getting into more debt with impulse purchases. Experts in mindset can be called in when required. But again, even mindset experts cannot help until you are 100% honest with yourself.

- List all expenses and income, assets and liabilities on a spreadsheet or use an app – that's up to you. Again, be honest. Don't be afraid of seeing yourself in the red. We can help you get back into the green.

- Track your spending. You can't see your results if you don't track your progress. (This sounds like Mark's personal trainer on this point.)

- Bring in a debt expert sooner rather than later. They know their stuff and 99.9% of the time they can help. John, our debt expert, recently saved one of our community members $55k in credit card debt. So, you see, it is worth making the phone call.

- Reduce your expenses and start to live within your means.

- Increase your income. There is no shame in working a second job. To us, it shows true commitment from you to achieve your goals.

- Look to use Uber or Air BnB, or similar, to increase income.

- Build a side business (see Part Three for some ideas).

Banking

To complement your debt reduction plan, look to set up your banking differently as well. First, create what we call a wealth account. This will only be used for investing, buying assets and creating other income streams. Each pay day, automatically transfer whatever you can afford or are comfortable with depositing. Just start. Most people say that they have nothing to invest with after paying their bills.

The way of the wealthy – pay yourself first

Here is a ninja trick to find some cash so you can start to build your wealth account. We believe that if you have a debt reduction plan and a wealth account going at the same time, it does speed things up.

If you rent or have a mortgage, what amount must your rent or mortgage go up per week for you to decide to move? Would you move if it went up by $50? If yes, then reduce it. If no, then increase it. Keep adjusting that figure until you find the largest number that you wouldn't move for. It costs a lot of money to move to a new house and most people wouldn't move for $20, $40, or even $100 a week. So, what's the biggest increase in rent you would tolerate? With that number, we have found you some money to invest into your wealth account. To make this work, you can tell yourself that the landlord or the bank has increased your payments. Have the "extra" payment directed to your wealth account.

The next ninja trick is to set up your wealth account so you cannot touch it easily. Remember, it is for investing, not for when the car breaks down or for the kids' school fees. You can set up another account like this for a rainy day if you want to. However, the wealth account must be used only to invest with once you hit the amount you want to start with. At time of writing (early 2019), we have access to investments where you can start with $100, so you don't need thousands to start.

When we did this, we made sure we had no ATM card, no internet access and no phone banking. There were no apps or tap-and-pay back then either. The bank's staff will do their best to sell you every single one of these services. **YOU MUST SAY NO** (yes, we're shouting again!). Also, have the branch at least 30 to 45 minutes' drive away from your work or home. That way it becomes a pain in the butt to get your money out and it stops you from impulse buying. Imagine saying, "Nice shoes, I'm going to drive 45 minutes one way, get my money out and drive 45 minutes back to buy them." 99% of the time you will not do that.

Once you become disciplined enough, you can add the account to your internet banking to make life easier for when you are ready to invest. If investing is new to you, then we have found this is the best way to ensure you don't lose focus or use your wealth account for anything but investing. We can honestly say that setting up our wealth account was the single most important step on our journey of creating financial independence. **Bar none.** It gave us a sense of paying ourselves first, as that is what wealthy people do. We would forget we had it until the statements came in the mail (yep, paper statements).

Speed savings

Speed savings is a term we came up with when companies such as Raiz (formerly Acorns) came onto the scene. It allows you to save money without trying and is not in a bank account that is easy to get to. Raiz rounds up your spending to the nearest $1, $2, $10, etc., when you connect your bank accounts to their service. For example, if you purchased a coffee for $4.50 and you instructed them to round up to the nearest dollar, they would deduct 50c from your account and then invest it for you. You have a choice of different "risk profiles" to invest in. You can do regular direct debit payments as well. We call it speed savings because, while it is technically an investment product, you have no real control of what companies they invest in as your funds go into a pool, and they invest according to your risk profile.

Pros:
- You hardly miss the amounts being deducted.
- The money is not in your account and can take five business days to get the funds returned.
- It really does speed up your savings so you can transfer it to your wealth account. A member of our community saved just over $7k in three months just by spending normally and rounding up to $20.

Cons:
- The balance can go down as it invested mainly in the share market.
- No control of the investment strategy in the purest form.

Case Study – Raiz

One of our members, John, set up a Raiz account, as he was interested in automatically saving and investing money into the market. He started direct debiting $115 every week from his account to Raiz. On top of this, he added the round up option (to the nearest dollar). Within the space of 6 months, he had grown his account from $0 to $5,500. From here, he withdrew $4,500 of this and allocated it to another investment. John is focused on continuing the process again, and again – hence speed savings.

Other options to speed save are:
- ABC Bullion: You can speed save (or invest, as we love gold and silver as an investment strategy) with a minimum $20 per week. This can be converted into physical gold or silver whenever you want. Check them out at www.abcbullion.com.au
- Amber: At time of writing, Amber is in beta mode and is very close to being available. It is like Raiz for the crypto space. Check them out at www.getamber.io

Secrets of the wealthy

Wealthy people do three things better than "poor" people.

1. They focus on their long-term goals.
2. They deny their short-term impulses.
3. They look for long term duplication.

Long-term goals

Wealthy people understand that becoming financially free does not happen overnight. It takes small and consistent steps to have more freedom and more choices. By staying focused on the long game, they end up getting there faster. Compounding is so powerful and the wealthy master this power better than anyone. If you purchased a $250 pair of shoes today, you are missing out on $16,553 in 30 years' time. That is how much the $250 would be worth if you invested with compound interest. Next time you go to buy these shoes, ask yourself, "Are these worth $16,553"? (P.S. Billie thinks you should still buy the shoes.)

Short term impulses

There is a reason why they put the chocolate bars at the counter in every supermarket. We impulse buy them. They generally have the highest profit margins. Most (and I do say most) of us don't say to ourselves, "I'm off to buy some chocolate today." And yet we end up with some. Not always, but often. Well, 60% of us do, as that is how many people are estimated to be overweight in Australia and the USA.

We know it's not just the chocolate to blame. Marketers understand the psychology of buyer behaviour more than anyone. That is their job. They know that impulse buying is a big part of your spending habits. In order to become wealthy, you will need to reduce your impulse buying.

I believe one trick we have implemented this year will work well. Our family can be lazy cooks. Billie thinks she can't cook (she can). I love to cook, but not all the time. We use Menulog or Uber Eats when we can't be bothered to cook. This adds up. So, this year, when we order instead of cooking, that money now comes out of our holiday account. Our goal is to have a white Christmas somewhere like New York. The kids are on board, and already we have seen a reduction of meals being delivered. To compound it, if we get close to ordering and we decide not to, whatever the cost of the food was going to be is added to our holiday account. Not only are we saving money, we are tricking our minds as well as adding money to our holiday account. Plus, it's much healthier on all fronts, right?

Long-term duplication

The third action wealthy people do better is long term duplication. In business, investing and health, they look to find what works and duplicate it.

Duplicating what works compounds their results. It allows them to consistently and constantly repeat successful systems. Quite often, non-wealthy people will do something once and will then look to do something different, even if it worked. Wealthy people are not afraid to use other people's systems. They do not need to reinvent the wheel in order to become wealthy. The system within this book works. If you apply the steps that relate to you and your situation, then you will be on your way to building lasting wealth, reducing stress and giving yourself more choices and freedom.

What short term denials will you execute to achieve your dreams? Will you stop buying takeaway this week so you can eat at any restaurant in the world in 10 years' time? Will you forgo those shoes today so that you can buy $1,000 shoes five years from now while in Paris, Rome or New York? Consistently changing your habits and mindset is the key to having the lifestyle you want.

Biggest takeaways, actions required and notes

_____
_____
_____
_____
_____
_____
_____
_____
_____
_____
_____
_____
_____
_____
_____
_____
_____
_____
_____
_____

Community experts case study – Tom & Jane

Here's another example of how our community members, experts in their fields, can help you get on the right track. Tom and Jane came to Sim Chan, founder of Smarter Investment Management, for advice.

Tom and Jane wanted to pay down their $425,000 mortgage faster. Sim was able to show them a strategy to reduce their loan term from 25 years down to 13 years, saving $204,000 in interest payments alone.

Sim worked with Tom and Jane to uncover the underlying challenges that had been stopping them from reducing their debt. Jane had a limiting belief about wealth and had been unconsciously self-sabotaging their progress by adding onto their debt whenever the debt reduction hit a self-imposed threshold.

They were able to reduce their debt down to $336,867 in 3 years. Once Tom turned 60, they would use his super to fast-track the debt reduction. However, Tom was diagnosed with Parkinson's disease. Tom was not keen on personal insurances and felt that the Life and Total & Permanent Disablement of $150,000 that he received from his super would be enough.

Luckily, Sim showed him the importance of protection and put in place a comprehensive insurance plan for both him and Jane. They were able to pay off their debt and his medical expenses. He is also receiving an income from his income protection policy. More importantly, they are still able to continue building their nest egg for their retirement, and have added another $559,000.

Sim Chan is a highly regarded, trusted financial adviser and wealth coach with her own financial planning practice, Smarter Investment Management, in Sydney. With her own journey from riches to rags to riches as her driving force, Sim is passionate about empowering clients and enabling them to control their finances with clarity and foresight.

Working in the financial services industry for the last 15 years, she has the knack of translating financial jargon into easy-to-follow strategies. One of her chief focuses is helping clients rid themselves of debt while building a nest egg for their future.

Sim links her knowledge of gaining financial security and freedom to the emotional hurdles that often stand in the way. Rather than list a countless number of humdrum 'must dos,' she encourages her clients to accept their situation without ignoring their dreams.

'When you know what you want to create, set powerful intentions on a daily basis. Intention is the starting point of every dream and aspiration.' — *Sim Chan*

PART TWO – BUILDING YOUR FINANCIAL INDEPENDENCE FORMULA

"There is nothing wrong with a 'know-nothing' investor who realises it. The problem is when you are a 'know nothing' investor but you think you know something."
— Warren Buffett

Once you have a debt reduction plan in place, it is time to start thinking about investing. But where do you start? Everyone is out to scam you, right? Wrong but, man, there are a lot of unscrupulous people out there with their own agendas. Trust is at an all-time low. We get it. We believe we have chosen the toughest niche to educate people in at this point in time.

We tell members of the International Academy of Wealth not to blindly trust us either. We must earn your trust. You must take responsibility to do your own research (DYOR) and your own due diligence (DD) on both of us, on the Academy, and on any of our experts that we trust and recommend. This applies to the strategies we educate people on as well. The last thing you should be saying is, "Well, if Mark has money in that strategy, it must be great." **NO**. Your Money Rules will be different to my Money Rules (more on that shortly).

Same goes with what our governments, banks, superannuation funds and insurance companies say. Don't trust them and what they say until you have DYOR and done your DD. We're not saying you shouldn't use their services. What we're saying is, take responsibility and consider what they are saying before deciding.

Let's look at some of the statements that have come from these institutions or governments in the past. We'll share our thoughts on them as we go.

Dispelling the myths around investing

Myth #1: "The government will look after us."

Not everything we have been taught is correct. In fact, on so many levels, we're being lied to, cheated by, and stolen from by big institutions and our governments.

No one seems to be heading to jail from these companies anytime soon, from looking at the recent financial Royal Commission reports. Why is that? Why is the government not looking after us? Why do they aim for the smaller fish to go after and crucify?

I don't know how anyone believe the governments are looking out for our interests when:

- Pension age is now 67 and moving to 70,
- Pensions are being reduced,
- Benefits are being reduced,
- Medical costs are increasing,
- Sale of prime food-producing land to China has increased from 1.4 million hectares to over 14 million hectares (and at what point will China want to protect their investment?),
- The bill for our politicians is over half a billion dollars ($506,000,000) per year and increasing. That's for both past and current politicians. That's around $2 million per politician, per year. That is just insane.

If you think the government's going to look after us all, you are kidding yourself.

Myth #2: "The higher the risk, the higher the return."

Where did this idea come from? Sure, in some cases this is true. However, with most opportunities that come across our desk, it's not the case at all. To us, the difference between risk levels comes down to the person's understanding of the opportunity and how much due diligence they have completed. This can reduce the risk while having a higher return.

Myth #3: "It sounds too good to be true."

Now, this is one that we find interesting. Again, where did this come from? If you take a bank here in Australia, for example, they made $26 billion AUD gross, or $9.2 billion in net profit. With 8 million customers, that's around $3,250 per customer. There's no way that this bank can make $9.2 billion in net profit on investments that make less than 10% per annum. It just doesn't happen. We know that they have other strategies that make way more than that, and yet, they're the ones who generally are saying "Sounds too good to be true."

Myth #4: "You've worked hard, buy it now and pay it off."

OK, it's not really an investing myth, however it stops 95% of people from investing. Who truly benefits from this myth? The banks — and they have you right where they've educated you. Think about it. They continuously advertise, "Have everything now, pay for it later" — and pay, you will. Remember the $38k credit card example that will take 141 years to pay off?

Myth #5: "Your money is safe in the bank."

Probably the most dangerous myth there is. It's 100% BS. Here's the deal. On 14 February 2018, a law was passed in Australia that allows banks to use your money to bail them out, should they get into trouble. They call it a 'bail-in'. The United States, Greece, Cyprus, and New Zealand also have similar laws. The part that really concerns me is that people think that their money is safe in a bank. It's not.

Moving on...

With these myths out of the way, we want to share why the current way we are educated to invest is setting us up for complete financial failure. There are several factors you need to consider. Who created the current investing system? Who is teaching the current investing system? If the current system worked, why have the stats around financial independence and retirement not changed in 35 years? Why do less than 5% of people retire financially comfortable?

Four reasons why your current investments strategies will wipe out any chance of financial independence

1: The world economy

You might be thinking, "I've read this first reason before." It's because you have. It was in a previous chapter — "The world is drowning in debt and taking you with it". We felt it was important enough to have its own chapter towards the front of the book. It is a major reason why the way you are investing now can wipe out any chance of your financial independence. It is worth reading the chapter again to fully understand the pain (or profit, now that you know this information) that is about happen.

2: Job security

In a number of countries around the world, the unemployment rate is high. Greece is at 20% unemployment, with Spain close behind at 16% and Italy at 10.9%. Australia is sitting at 5.29% for 2018. Governments tend to manipulate these figures, depending on what they need at the time — so it's just trying to figure out what figures from which sources to believe.

Private sector jobs have been declining on a regular basis for the last 10 years or so. The labour force participation rate has also been at its lowest since 1978. The average household income for Americans has been declining. We personally see the effects of this because we use the services from a company called Upwork, where freelancers can offer their own rates.

Quite often, we're getting quotes from people in America and they're price-matching places like the Philippines and other less affluent economies. We would assume that the Americans would have to charge more because of the cost of living, but that's not necessarily the case. They have to take what they can get too! One of our team members we found via Upwork is in the Philippines and is coming up to his 10th anniversary with us.

Labour can now be accessed from anywhere, so your job, especially in service-based businesses, can be done from anywhere in the world. Graphic design, accounting and bookkeeping are among those fields being taken over by developing nations such as India, China and other emerging markets, as they have a plentiful supply of cheap (and qualified) labour. There are so many places that you can get quality employees or contractors now, for a fraction of the price.

You've also got robots doing work of hundreds, if not thousands, of people. Spyce Kitchen, a restaurant in Boston, Massachusetts, has the whole kitchen run by robotics. So even "safe" jobs such as chefs are under attack. In fact, there are already more than 3 million workers globally that are being supervised by a robo-boss.

Take Uber, for example. They have disrupted the taxi industry and have brought joy to my world (I never really liked taxi driver's high fees and the 10% surcharge to use your credit card). Uber is now also highly advanced in their driverless car program. At some point, when we all are used to taking an Uber, it will be a driverless Uber car instead. We have driverless trucks already on the road in parts of the USA and Europe. All the transport industry will be affected.

Baby boomers are leaving employment or retiring, and they're not being replaced, or they're being replaced by computers, robots or artificial intelligence. Effectively, we're having our kids go through university and rack up massive amounts of student debt, and the jobs they are learning the skills for might not be there in the future. It is a significant amount of money for our kids to owe when they start their working lives. The real concern is that if any of the kids go bankrupt, all the other debts *except* for their student loans can be wiped out, so they can't even start again with a clean slate. They owe this money until it is paid off or they die — hard truth, end of story.

When you look at job security as one of the main reasons why your wealth can be wiped out, it's just alarming. Even in the legal profession, where you would assume you would need actual people to work, there's IBM's super-computer Watson. Watson is already literally the smartest lawyer on the planet, and he's a computer!

All of this has been designed to enslave us till we die, to trick us into thinking we must work for 60 years and be grateful for the job they let us stay in. Slavery – it works better when you don't tell them.

3: Superannuation

To us, superannuation is a fancy word for tax. We will show you why. The government needs to control your super. And their plan is already underway. It started way back in 2007, and we could spend... In fact, we've done 60- to 90-minute presentations on this topic alone. But here's the short version.

Australia has $2.5 trillion in assets within the superannuation system. The forecast for 2035 is $9.5 trillion. This isn't us making up numbers. Deloitte Australia actuaries and consultants have modelled it using comprehensive demographic and financial analytical tools. We could turn around and say they have made up these numbers as well, however they've got a lot more money to spend to make sure these numbers correct. Compounding within the superannuation system is easier to do than in most other scenarios, as it cannot be touched for 10, 20 or 30 years. Hitting $9.5 trillion in assets is achievable.

On the other side of the coin, though, the current national debt is $714 billion[3]. As a country, we owe way more than that, but let's just focus on our mates at the government. Using the same analytical tools, we're looking at around $10 trillion by 2026 and — like we have mentioned before and will keep saying over and over — there's the compounding effect. You'll find that when you compound something, it does start to really speed up over time. That's why when you look at this — and yes, we only owe $714 billion now — $10 trillion is not out of the picture. If we keep spending the way we are, our government will hit that figure.

To give you some perspective. If all the government was charged is 2% per annum interest on that $10 trillion, that's $200 billion a year that they will have to find just for the interest payment alone, which is $547 million dollars **every single day**.

It's going to get harder for the government to get rid of their deficit and start being back in profit. Just in case you think that they will be able to turn it around and become profitable, there are more reasons why the government won't be turning a profit any time soon:

---

[3] Check out http://www.australiandebtclock.com.au/clocks for the current national debt.

- 77% of people over 65 receive some form of pension, whether it's a part pension or a full pension.
- When we have a look at today's revenue, 57% of government's revenue goes on health and welfare. This same sort of statistic applies to pretty much all western economies.
- We're not far away from having one person working for every three people on some form of social security.
- If we add the interest payments as well, we're looking at 61% of the government's revenue going to health, welfare and interest payments.
- This leaves only got 39% to actually run the country.

Can you see why the government needs to take control of your super? We've got $2 trillion. The government is in debt to the tune of $714 billion. If the government cashed out our super, they would have just under $1.4 trillion sitting in their bank account. If all they did was just use our superannuation and pay us a pension out of that until we die, they would still be well and truly ahead of the game. We'll be brutally honest — if we were the government, we would be eyeing off your super like there's no tomorrow!

They've already started to control it and, like we said, they started this many, many years ago. Back in 2007, we saw the first real sign that they wanted to come after our money. They brought in what they call My Super, which is just a default fund. Basically, if you don't have your own superannuation fund — whether it's industry or retail or self-managed — you would be put into these My Super ones. They have relatively low fees, not many options to choose from, and they are rapidly growing. A lot of people don't really care about their super. They don't understand it. We've had some people say that they didn't even know it was their money. So, the government has pulled these people into this My Super thing, and we believe that that's where the government will start when they take control of it.

They are already taking our money now. If you haven't been in touch with your current superannuation fund for some time, then that money goes to the actual government. The government should really put that money that's yours onto their balance sheet as a liability — because it's not their money, it's ours. However, what they're doing is putting it into their cash flow and treating it as income. That is just, on all levels of accounting, completely wrong — let alone morally and ethically.

If you wanted to go into https://www.budget.gov.au/ and get right into the guts of things, about 10 pages deep you can see that in the 2013-14 year they made $403 million, and they were projecting $4.8 billion over the four years to 2016-17.

What used to happen was super ended up being classified as "lost" if the balance was $2,000 or less with no contact between the owner and the super fund managers for four years. Then it would go to the ATO. However, they've changed the rules now, and it has been increased to $6,000 and two years. If you've got $6k or less, and you haven't been in touch with your superannuation fund for a couple of years, then they must, by law, transfer it to the government. Two years and one day — gone, straight to the government.

You can get it back, though. Don't think that it's lost forever. They will give it back to you. However, the thing that makes us laugh is: how can it be lost? They tend to find us when we owe tax, and very quickly, so why can't they find us to give us our super back? Most super funds have our actual tax file number!

The Turnbull government — well, he's no longer there — hoovered up more than $2 billion of inactive superannuation. The current Morrison government is now raking in $1.1 billion from inactive accounts into the underlying cash balance over the next four years, and they will gain an extra $166 million from taxes. This was updated in June 2018. That, to me, is crazy. It cannot be stressed enough how frustrating that is for us.

If you think you can take out a lump sum from your super when you retire, you might be in for a big shock. Deputy Secretary to the Treasury John Lonsdale stated at a private function that, "[people] will most likely be stopped from taking their superannuation as a lump sum and will have to access it through a structured self-funded pension." So even if they don't take it off us and control it, they're going to tell you that you cannot pull out a lump sum and buy that caravan, or pay the mortgage down, or buy this and that, or go on that world trip that you've always wanted and were waiting to retire so you could afford it. They're going to turn around and say, "No, you have to fund your own pension and pay yourself $20k-odd a year until you die."

Another thing: our mate Scott Morrison, when he was the Minister for Social Services — this week he's our Prime Minister as well — also told Fairfax Media, "The purpose of providing tax incentives to encourage people to build up their super is so they can draw down on it in their retirement, not maintain it as a capital pool to be passed on as an inheritance."

What he's basically saying, in a roundabout way, is that it's going to be an "expiry on death" clause. If you don't use it all, they're going to make it so that you only pay yourself a minimum amount in case you live 50 or 60 years after retirement. But they're also saying that when you don't use it, it's now the government's, and you can't pass it on as an inheritance. That, to us, is just so wrong on so many levels. But, like we said, this is all our opinion — based on some serious research.

If you think that you're going to be safe with an industry fund, we can assure you that, even as friendly as they seem, the industry funds have what they call trustee companies — and most trustee companies are owned by private individuals, private companies, or unions, depending on the structure.

Here is an example of how they're structured. A while ago, UniSuper quietly changed the rules and, at Christmas, they sent it in a 30-page document about your super. We don't know about you, but we haven't met anybody who has honestly said that they would have read a 30-page financial document during the holiday season.

They changed the rules to let the employer off the hook. Clause 34 of the trust deed originally said, "If we don't have the cash to fund the member's retirement, then the employer will make up the difference."

Now, with UniSuper, the employers are universities. When you dig deeper, the trustees are also the universities. To us, that's a massive conflict of interest. They change a clause to basically protect the employer, not the members of the super fund — and the trustees and the employers are the same entities.

This is one of the largest industry funds in the country. They've got $70 billion under management, and over 400,000 members. This one change means that if the super fund doesn't have enough money, over 100,000 members could lose their retirement income.

Will a self-managed super fund (SMSF) "save" me? Not 100%, however we believe self-managed super funds will be targeted last because they are not the low-hanging fruit.

With a SMSF you have greater control than you do with any other type of super fund. They are inexpensive to set up (provided the balance to admin fee ratio is worth it) and you do not need an accountant or financial planner to do so. We do believe, however, that you should use an expert to help with the taxes and compliance.

We know that a lot of people think that we're crazy — tinfoil hats — when we talk about this stuff and that's fine, but the trend is clear. Taxes are rising, governments are spending more, and debts are getting higher. The budget deficits are also rising. An easy way for an Australian government to cover some, if not all, of these costs would be to dip into the $2 trillion in Australian superannuation. Like we said, be open-minded because not everything we're getting told is correct, and we really would love for you to do your own homework (and share it with us!).

How do you like my tinfoil hat?

Case Study

One client, who happens to fit into our regular demographic, has had life-altering experiences since joining iFlip. During 2017, her money was managed by one of the big name financial advisory firms. The money was her inheritance and was a little above $1 million USD, and she was relying on this money to provide her an income for the rest of her life.

Most of us know that the market — specifically the S&P 500 — had a record year in 2017, and her advisor had her money fully invested in the stock market. The S&P had a 20% return in 2017. Our customer's portfolio had a 6% return, which means she underperformed the market by -14%. She also paid over $30,000 in combined *fees* in 2017. In 2018, the S&P did -6.35% for those invested for the year. The software produced 6.05%, beating the market by +12%. And the fees for one year of using the software were $948.

This customer now has all the extra money she was paying in fees earning money, instead of going to the financial institution that was "managing" her money. Over time, this will produce more money than she will spend — thereby creating legacy wealth and setting up not just her but her children and, if done right, their children. That is much more than just life changing, that's legacy creating.

4: AI and the rise of the machine trader

Let's go back to 1996 and Garry Kasparov, the chess grandmaster. Garry beat Deep Blue, the best computer that IBM could create to play chess. He smashed this computer and he was very confident. But one year later, he lost. Over the following 27 years, very few — if any — humans have been able to beat the best chess computers. The significance of this has been lost on most people.

This is the moment in time when we should've stood up and taken notice of what the future holds. Some of us did, and others didn't. The key to this is the need to understand that computers are far more intelligent than most of us humans right now. There is a point in time, called the singularity, where they believe that computers will be more intelligent than every human on the planet.

Where we're heading with this is from an investment point of view. Susan Polgár is a six-time grandmaster and a chess coach. A very clever lady. She says that computers do all the retreating because they're not slaves to human nature — humans don't like to admit a mistake unless they really have to. From a trading perspective, the amount of people we've seen lose trades and lose all their capital rather than taking a smaller loss is ridiculous. As humans, our egos get in the way of a retreating trade. We stay until the bitter end. And all is lost rather than, like we said, just taking a smaller loss and learn to fight another day.

Not only do you have to fight your own human emotions with pinpoint accuracy when it comes to trading and deal with fear, greed and ego — you now also have to fight the high-speed computers. You've got MIT grads creating mathematical algorithms that us mere mortals would never understand.

Take this quote from Jon Kafton — founder of Cloud9Trader, an automated online trading site: "*Humans consistently underperform because they have emotional interference. Algo [algorithm] trading formalizes your strategy upfront and sets clear boundaries on your risk exposure.*" That, to us, says a lot. When you understand this and partner with expert advisors or high-speed computers and bots, you're going to make some serious profits moving forward.

So-called "gurus" who sell $5k, $10k and $35k "learn how to trade" programs from the stage don't tell you this. They tell you that, for an hour a day, or an hour a week, you'll learn the trade. Guy Langford, a trusted trader we know and a member of our community, can dispel those myths. One of the things these gurus don't tell you is that 84% of all stock orders traded are now executed by high frequency computers. Only 16% are done by human traders. We would love to know — out of that 16%, how many are brand-new traders, newbies? And how many are actual professional traders and do that for a living?

Bloomberg is one of our favourite places to get financial information. They're upfront and have a full understanding of exactly what's going on. When you understand that, it's incredible. If you're wanting to learn how to trade — whether it's shares, forex, or commodities such as gold and silver and oil — you have to really beat everybody just to win, let alone to make a profit and become financially independent.

If you add in the people who have access to the strategies that we have access to, the number of minefields that you have to go through is crazy. If you don't have the lay of the land, it's going to be virtually impossible for you to make money.

You need to understand, the exciting part of this is that you now have this information and you can do what you want with it. Without knowing all these facts, there will only be one winner if you're going to go spend $35k on a training course — and that's the guru at the front of the room, while you end up alone and in the dark. It's pretty painful. You'll end up in more debt if you're taking out a loan to get the course, and you'll be burning yourself out looking at your computer screen, just trying to get your $35k back.

Why are we telling you this?
We needed to share all this because, if you truly understand these four big reasons, they have the potential to wipe out any chance of you being financially independent. Three of them are a bit of a downer. The AI one is exciting when you understand that there are trading bots, EAs, and traders that you can mirror trade, without knowing how to trade yourself, and the profits can be fantastic. We've been trying to avoid saying how much the returns are. But they are absolutely staggering. We believe that when you have all the information at your fingertips, what you do with it is up to you. But the more knowledge you have, the more power you have as well.

We believe that most old strategies are tied with the old system, and the old system is not working so well. Strategies like buy-and-hold shares, properties that are negatively geared and the reliance on one income source per person are completely over. The more income streams you have, the better. We'll rephrase that —we do believe you can have too many income streams. The best thing you can do is focus on certain ones within your area of interest and risk inclination or aversion. We recommend diversification within diversification — having multiple property passive income streams, multiple forex passive income streams, multiple share passive income streams — rather than having say 30, 40, 50 different streams of income. We would rather have eight to 12 quality passive income streams coming in, year in year out, than having to manage loads of them.

Our reliance on effectively bankrupt trading partners (China, Japan, USA) is going to almost wipe out Australia when they fold. Reliance on the government to look after you in retirement is not going to work. Overpriced trading courses are not telling you the whole truth. People are spending money on pipe-dreams and 99.9% won't get their money back, let alone live their dream life.

The relationship is now stronger and more profitable between humans and computers than in the past. If you can understand and utilise AI, you'll have the tools to become future-investment ready and build your own financial independence formula. That's what we are excited about.

While looking at everything that you do and that you start to build with your investments, you might want to build your active income so that you can reduce your debts and/or expenses.

If you need $60k per year to become financially independent, you don't need to go out and find a strategy that's going to pay you $60k a year instantly. Imagine if you could just take an extra day off a year, and then a day off a month, and then a day off a week. Chunk it right down so that the goals are far more achievable to you. Build it gradually. Rome wasn't built in a day, and your financial independence won't be either.

NOTE: other factors that will have an impact on your wealth are tax and capital control. We spoke briefly before about capital control, with banks now being able to take your money if they need it, and the government's plan to control your super. Tax also has the ability to reduce your wealth over time.

Biggest takeaways, actions required and notes

THE FINANCIAL INDEPENDENCE FORMULA

AI + PI + LTI > FE + IE + LE

Everybody will have a different formula, or at least different figures within this formula. Some can become financially free on $35k a year while others are aiming for $500k a year or more. That's OK. It's your life, build it your way. Only you can decide what type of lifestyle you want to live.

We like to use the analogy of airplane travel. What type of lifestyle do you want to live? Economy, premium economy, business class or first class? Personally, I want none of it — I want a private jet! The choice is yours. The choice can also be a lot closer than you think.

What an economy lifestyle may look like in Sydney would be a first-class lifestyle in Bali. $200k per year will give you an economy to premium economy lifestyle on Sydney's northern beaches, while $200k in the south of Spain would be close to first class. Does that make sense? Now, we're not saying you should leave, not at all! What we are saying is that you could get your passive income streams to a point where, if you decided you'd had enough of working, you could move to Bali. It gives you a sense of freedom. $15k a year will give you a very comfortable lifestyle in Bali.

Of course, the government and the banking system need us to stay in economy or better yet in cargo class.

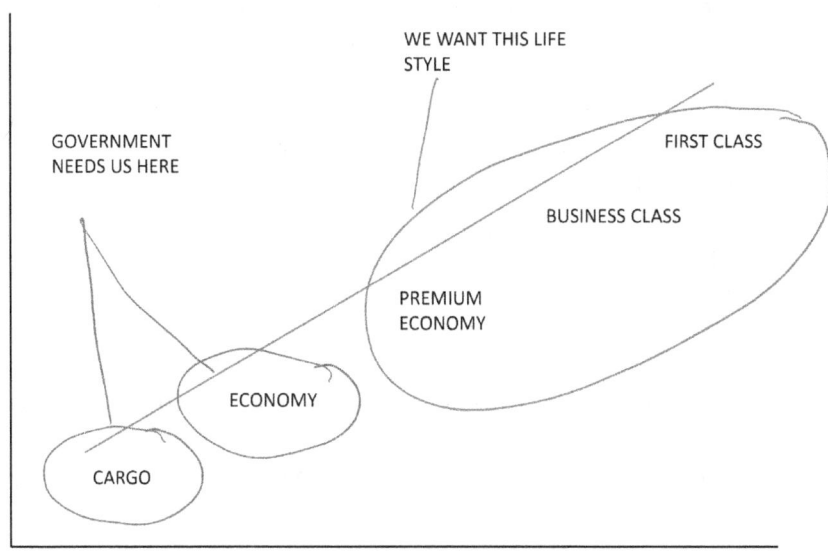

Let's look at the different parts to the financial independence formula.

AI — ACTIVE INCOME

Our definition of active income is: "if you have to turn up to a certain place of business to create an income, then this is active income". If the law states that you can only work from one country, it is active income.

Types of AI include anything that is paid by an employer for a job based in a specific place, or if you run a business and you need to turn up somewhere specific to run it.

PI — PASSIVE INCOME

Passive income is kind of an oxymoron. We believe there is no such thing as passive income in the truest sense. All income streams need some time spent reviewing and managing. However, it is the only income stream that gives you complete financial independence. Active income and laptop income both require you to spend your time building and managing it. Financial independence is about choice. If you choose to work an active income or a laptop income stream, then that is your choice. Right now, though, 99.9% of people must rely on active income or a laptop income stream. Passive is where real independence is.

Types of PI include bank interest (whatever that is!), dividends from shares or private companies, rental income from properties, and income from trading activities that you don't personally handle.

LTI — LAPTOP INCOME

Laptop income is where you can work anywhere in the world and create money. My role in the International Academy of Wealth, for example, is a laptop income stream. We can work anywhere in the world and deliver the value that we do. Our investor Base Camps can be held around the world, so it is a true laptop income.

Types of LTI can be coaching, online memberships, share trading, currency trading, etc.

Now let's head over to the other side of the equation.

FE — FIXED EXPENSES

Fixed expenses should be limited to covering the basic human needs such as food, clothing and shelter — however, in today's modern society, categories such as transport and internet can be added here. Remember, this is *your* financial independence formula. You add your expenses where they make the most sense to you.

Here is an example. To me, car expenses are a lifestyle expense, especially when you live in a city with amazing public transport. We currently live in Sydney, which has everything — buses, trains, and ferries to take us around. We don't need a car. We have our car expenses under lifestyle. If we lived in the country or in a city where we had to have a car for either of us to create an income stream, it would fall under fixed expenses. But if you just need a normal car to get to work and you have gone out and spent $120k on a car... Mate, get real, that's a lifestyle expense.

Types of fixed expenses are rent or mortgage, power or gas, phone (to some extent), food (the basics only – Menulog, Pizza Hut, etc., are lifestyle).

NOTE: Too many people have too many fixed expenses. This can be due to too many lifestyle expenses that they have then converted to debt via personal loans or credit cards. They then have a fixed expense every month that they now must cover. Generally, they have not reduced their lifestyle expenses either.

IE — INVESTMENT EXPENSES

To me, investment expenses cover anything that helps you build an income stream in the passive income part of the equation. If you have expenses in running your active income or your laptop income, you would have factored that in already. You may also factor in the investment expenses on, say, a rental property and just add the net amount to the equation. For example, if you have a property that returns $35k per year, and the expenses — such as interest on the loan, property management, rates, insurances, etc. — comes to $30k per year, you can do one of two things. You can add the difference of $5k to your passive income part of the equation, or you can add $35k to the passive income part and $30k to the investment expenses part. They will both work out to be the same answer.

Types of investment expenses are any that relate to investment properties, education on an investment strategy you are currently in, community membership, brokerage fees, etc.

LE — LIFESTYLE EXPENSES

Good old lifestyle expenses. "Keeping up with the Joneses". It is usually the section that people have back to front. Not even back to front, because, as your wealth grows, your fixed expenses as a percentage of your overall income and net worth decreases. A friend of ours says, "Spend your profits on lifestyle, not your income". We love what he is trying to say. Most people will spend income they don't have on the lifestyle they can't afford, to impress people that don't matter.

When building your financial independence spending plan, your lifestyle expenses may be higher than your fixed expenses. However, before you get there, you do need to ensure your lifestyle expenses are as low as they can be while still having "a life". You need to live for today and plan for tomorrow. You can do both, but you can't do both if you just spend, spend, spend money that you do not have.

Types of lifestyle expenses include some food choices, clothing, travel, holidays, the latest phone every year, new cars (a used car is fine 99.9% of the time), concerts, dining out and shoes (Billie!).

Let's extend the car example a bit more. Say you spend $500 on car expenses. That includes the car payment, insurance, gas, and the occasional repair. $500 per month compounded at 8% over 20 years is almost $300,000 (factoring out taxes and inflation). We live in a car-oriented society because we have been educated to be. The type of car you own can be a status symbol, and public transportation is robust in only a few cities. We feel the need to own a car, but no longer do we need to. There are plenty of alternatives that you can look at. Run the numbers and see which one is going to give you the results long-term.

A lot of what we are covering, or the language we use, will be very new and that's OK. The formula above is simple to follow when you understand more about financial wealth, abundance, income, expenses assets and liabilities. This is part of building your foundations of wealth and building your financial independence. Increasing your knowledge around these matters is the beginning of the journey and will be part of the journey until you leave this world. Remember, anyone can become financially free. Being able to stay there is financial independence. So, let's cover some topics that will get you to become financially free, then allow you to stay financially independent.

FOUNDATIONS OF WEALTH

At some point in our lives, we would have heard or read the story of the three little pigs. Just to recap, the fairytale goes like this. Three little pigs decide to build a house each to protect themselves from the big bad wolf. The first one grabs the first material he sees and build his house with straw. He then sits back and drinks a beer (OK, I might be adding my own twists to this story). The second takes a bit more time, goes into the woods and ends up building his house with sticks. He sits back, puts on Netflix and grabs a beer. The third pig plans his house once he understands what the dangers are. He chooses the right location, builds solid foundations and he decides to use bricks. It did take him a bit longer, but he is now sitting back and relaxing with the air-con going, beer in the fridge and whiskey in the cupboard.

Now, the big bad wolf is getting a bit hungry. He comes across the first pig who built his house with straw. You know the story, so I'll cut a few corners here. The wolf huffs and puffs the first two little pigs' houses down. They run off to their brother's house and they live safely with him. **BROTHER PIG IS NOT A LONG-TERM BACK-UP PLAN.** He will kick you out eventually.

If we look at our finances as our house, we want to build as solid a financial house as we can. The big bad wolf is the system, governments, financial institutions, and people who want to sue you because they have an entitlement mentality. Do you want to build your financial house with straw, sticks or bricks? I'm hoping you said bricks. To build it as strong as possible, we need to have solid foundations. Below is what we believe is required for solid foundations so you can build your financial house with bricks.

End Game

You can't fire an arrow and call whatever it hits the target. You need something to aim for. You need to build out your End Game. This covers your spending plan and your net worth. This is not your run-of-the-mill goal setting. Most of the BS out there is too fluffy and, frankly, it doesn't work.

Writing down "I want to travel lots" also won't work. How are you going to pay for all that travel? Where is the income going to come from? "The universe will provide." Come on! It doesn't work that way. Without a doubt, you will get better results when you visualise your financial independence lifestyle, but sitting back and expecting the universe to provide is setting you up for failure. Even the universe needs you to get off your butt and take action. It reminds me of an old joke where a priest keeps complaining to God that he never wins lotto. One day God has enough and says to the priest, "Help me out here and buy a ticket."

You need a ticket in the game to have any chance of winning. So, when you are writing down your ideal lifestyle or your ideal financial independence lifestyle, you need to include:
- what type of income you will have: e.g. Active, Passive or Laptop;
- how much income you will get from each section;
- the types of income within the section: e.g. dividends, social trading, etc.;
- a complete list of your expenses broken into the three sub groups – fixed, investment and lifestyle;
- and what your net worth will look like.

See how they all interlink together? Add feeling to it, give it some soul!

By being very clear on your financial independence formula, it allows the universe to help you to achieve the desired lifestyle, backed by the required assets and income.

In the space below, start writing down the types of income and expenses you would like to achieve when you are financially free. Don't worry, this is just an example. When you get the Ultimate Wealth Acceleration Plan spreadsheet, it will be it A LOT easier. An example could be: share dividends = $8,700 or social trading = $34,589.

Active Income (AI)

_____
_____
_____
_____

Passive Income (PI)

_____
_____
_____
_____
_____
_____
_____

Laptop Income (LI)

_____
_____
_____
_____
_____
_____
_____

Total: _____

Now, write down what your future expenses will be. Remember that this is the life you want to lead, so go for it. This creates the reality of how much income you will need to live it. Examples could be: holidays – business class = $14,500, holidays – economy = $7890, rent for 4 months of the year = $25,800. This is your future life – build it your way.

Fixed Expenses (FE)

_____
_____
_____
_____
_____
_____
_____

Investment expenses (IE)

_____
_____
_____
_____
_____
_____

Lifestyle expenses (LE)

_____
_____
_____
_____
_____
_____
_____
_____
_____
_____

Total: _____

Future Net Investable Income (income minus expenses):

Now, write down what your assets and liabilities will look like. Again, there's a good chance this will change over time – however, we need something to aim for. Your assets will need to marry up with what income you have written down. No point in stating you earn $10k a year from dividends if your balance sheet doesn't show any holdings in shares.

Assets

_____
_____
_____
_____
_____
_____
_____
_____
_____
_____

Total assets: _____

Liabilities

_____
_____
_____
_____
_____
_____
_____
_____
_____

Total liabilities: _____

Future net worth (assets minus liabilities): _____

Starting point

Now you have an idea of where you want to go. It will change. In fact, it may change the minute you finish this book and that's OK. Be flexible, yet firm, with your goals. This will help you in the long run.

It's time for you to find out exactly where you are. This is your starting point. If you did the exercise in the debt reduction section, it's just a matter of copying it here. To start our journey to financial freedom and then financial independence, one must know the point at which they will start. Your starting point fluctuates every day – depending on what you spend your money on, how your investments are going and your debt levels. In every part of the foundations, reviews need to be carried out to ensure they are still solid and/or relevant with your goals. Complete the exercise below. Again, we get you to write it down to help cement the learnings. Remember, when moving forward, there are easier ways ahead to do all of this.

Fixed Expenses (FE)

_____
_____
_____
_____
_____
_____
_____
_____
_____

Investment Expenses (IE)

_____
_____
_____
_____
_____

Lifestyle Expenses (LE)

_____
_____
_____
_____
_____
_____
_____
_____
_____
_____
_____

Total: _____

Net Investable Income (income minus expenses):

_____

Assets

_____
_____
_____
_____
_____
_____
_____
_____
_____
_____
_____
_____
_____

Total assets: _____

Liabilities

_____
_____
_____
_____
_____
_____
_____
_____
_____
_____
_____

Total liabilities: _____

Current net worth (assets minus liabilities): _____

Net investable income and net investable capital

Once you have completed your starting point, this will give you two figures of interest: your net investable income and your net investable capital. Both are required for you to make decisions on what you can and cannot do, and what priorities you need to put in place to get you to the financial freedom point, then on to financial independence. It will also help you identify what strategies (both debt reduction and investment) you can employ straight away. Should one or both of these figures be a negative number, please reach out ASAP – the faster we fix the leaks, the faster we can get you on track to where you want to be. A couple of times in our lives, we have had to start way behind the start line. If you think of a 100-metre race, we were still in the changing rooms when the race started. But we still got into the race because we had taken the action needed. What you do with the positive numbers in your net investable income and net investable capital will be discussed in Money Rules in Part Three of this book.

Financial freedom point

This is the point where your active income (from a source that you truly want to be doing) plus your passive income, plus your laptop income **(AI + PI + LI)** is greater than your expenses **(FE + IE + LE)**. This is where you can, should you want to, tell your boss or your clients you are out. It is not, however, the point where you are financially independent. This takes years of continuing education on investment strategies, asset protection, tax strategies, business building, multiple streams of income, etc.

Debt control plan

No need to spend much time on this, as we covered everything you needed in the "Getting out of debt" section. Review what you have put in place monthly, quarterly or yearly – it's up to you. Just have a debt management plan in place. Even if you have no consumer debt (e.g. credit cards, personal loans car loans), start to pay down your investment and/or business debt. The less debt you have, the more net investable income you have, which allows you to invest more, which gives you more net investable income, and so on. This gives you a snowball effect in the right direction.

Money Rules

Yeah, it does! This is one of the most important parts of your foundations – having Money Rules. They need to be a little flexible, but not that flexible that you just do whatever it is that you want with your money. They should cover all areas of your spending and investing. We don't like to give too many examples as we find people tend to get lazy and just use them instead of creating their own. You need to own them or they will not work for you. We get that most people don't like having rules imposed on them – we *totally* get that. This is different, you're creating them for yourself to help improve your financial future. We can give you strategies that will put dollars in your pocket but without having Money Rules in place, the extra money could put you in a worse position than before. Create categories that you will have your Money Rules in and then start to build your rules. For example, one of our Money Rules is we never take credit cards to seminars. This will stop any chance of running to the back of the room and impulse-buying a course that we may not use. If the speaker wants our money, we are pretty sure he will give us the same deal the next day, once we have thought about it.

You've probably seen it stated before, especially if you know us at the International Academy of Wealth, that one of the reasons wealthy people success-fully achieve their financial freedom is because they write and implement Money Rules. It's that simple. We're not saying it's the only reason, but it is definitely one of them.

Below will give you an idea about formulating and implementing your own Money Rules into your life. By doing this, you will ensure greater success in achieving financial independence and escaping the "System", which people have been (unknowingly) educated into.

You might ask, "What are Money Rules?" Money Rules are designed by you to ensure you have greater congruency with the money you have and the decisions behind how you spend it. They ensure you are making the best decision for you and your End Game. For example, most people who write Money Rules almost always will have one of their rules as "Spend less than I earn in income." Now this rule may be a 'no-brainer', but you would be surprised just how many people are out there spending beyond their income. It's scary, actually. But this is where, as we mentioned above, people have been educated into the system. They use credit cards, store credits, pay-later systems, etc. These things all ensure you are spending more than you earn. Do you see what we mean?

As with our goals, needs, values, lives, etc., we are all different. We may have similarities but that is all they are. Our Money Rules will differ greatly or slightly from yours, and "theirs". This why we do not tell you what Money Rules you should have. It just wouldn't be right and, more than likely, not congruent to your life and your goals.

Some points for you to consider:
- Be open and honest with what your current spending habits are.
- Be ready to change the habits that are incongruent with your life and financial success.
- Refer to your goals – these will help you focus with your Money Rules.
- You may already be great with your money, Money Rules will only support this further.
- Money Rules are your guide to assisting you with incongruent habits that are limiting your financial success.
- Money Rules are designed to assist you when you are making financial decisions in investing, loans, purchases, major expenses, etc.
- Money Rules will assist your confidence level when making a decision with your money/purchase. You can refer to them if you are feeling a little out of control in a financial situation.
- Money Rules will help to keep you on track with your goals.

You will be surprised just how quickly, and easily, you will begin to make decisions based around your Money Rules. Before too long, you will be saying, "Yes, it fits my Money Rules," or "No, that does not fit my Money Rules." The cool thing around Money Rules is some are fluid and will change as your financial situation does. Some rules will stay in place, though.

Before you get started, we would like to point out a common mistake people make when creating Money Rules. They create their Money Rules for their future selves and future financial situation. While this works to a point, it will inevitably have you come unstuck.

Let's get started.

Money Rules – Spending: Daily Living

Think about your current spending habits for your daily living expenses. How do you make decisions when it comes to spending? Remember to be open and honest. Write as much as you can. This exercise is designed to help you get clarity around your spending habits.

_____
_____
_____
_____
_____
_____
_____
_____

Has the above helped or hindered your financial progress? How?

_____
_____
_____
_____
_____
_____
_____
_____

What would you like your spending habits around Daily Living to be?

_____
_____
_____
_____
_____
_____
_____
_____

Consider your answers to the above questions and formulate your new Daily Living Money Rules. Write them "as now", as if you are already doing it: e.g. "I pay my bills on time every time to avoid any late fees", "I follow a budget to ensure I have enough money every month for my daily living expenses".

My Money Rules for Daily Living expenses:
_____
_____
_____
_____
_____
_____
_____

Money Rules – Spending: Major Purchases

Think about your current spending habits on Major Purchases. How do you make decisions when it comes to spending? Remember to be open and honest. Write as much as you can.
_____
_____
_____
_____
_____
_____
_____
_____

Has the above helped or hindered your financial progress? How?
_____
_____
_____
_____
_____

What would you like your spending habits around Major Expenses to be?

_____
_____
_____
_____
_____
_____
_____

Consider your answers to the above questions and formulate your new Major Purchases Money Rules. Write them "as now", as if you are already doing it: e.g. "I only pay cash for Major Purchases", "I only buy Major Purchases when all my other expenses have been paid first".

My Money Rules for spending on Major Expenses:

_____
_____
_____
_____
_____
_____
_____
_____

Money Rules – Spending: Holidays and Travel

Think about your current spending habits on Holidays and Travel. How do you make decisions when it comes to spending? Remember to be open and honest. Write as much as you can.

_____
_____
_____

Has the above helped or hindered your financial progress? How?

What would you like your spending habits around Holidays and Travel to be?

Consider your answers to the above questions and formulate your Holidays and Travel Money Rules. Write them "as now", as if you are already doing it: e.g. "I only pay for holidays and travel when I have enough money in my specific bank account", "I always buy travel insurance for my overseas holidays to ensure no out-of-pocket expenses if should something arise".

My Money Rules for spending on Holidays and Travel expenses:

Money Rules – Spending: Health, Fitness & General Wellbeing

Think about your current spending habits on Health, Fitness & General Wellbeing. How do you make decisions when it comes to spending? Remember to be open and honest. Write as much as you can.

Has the above helped or hindered your financial progress? How?

What would you like your spending habits around HFGW to be?

Other areas you may consider are:
- Charity and donations
- Self-education and development
- Receiving lump sum payments
- Investing in property
- Investing in shares
- Investing in...

This little flowchart shows you just how quickly and effectively you can use your Money Rules to make spending decisions:

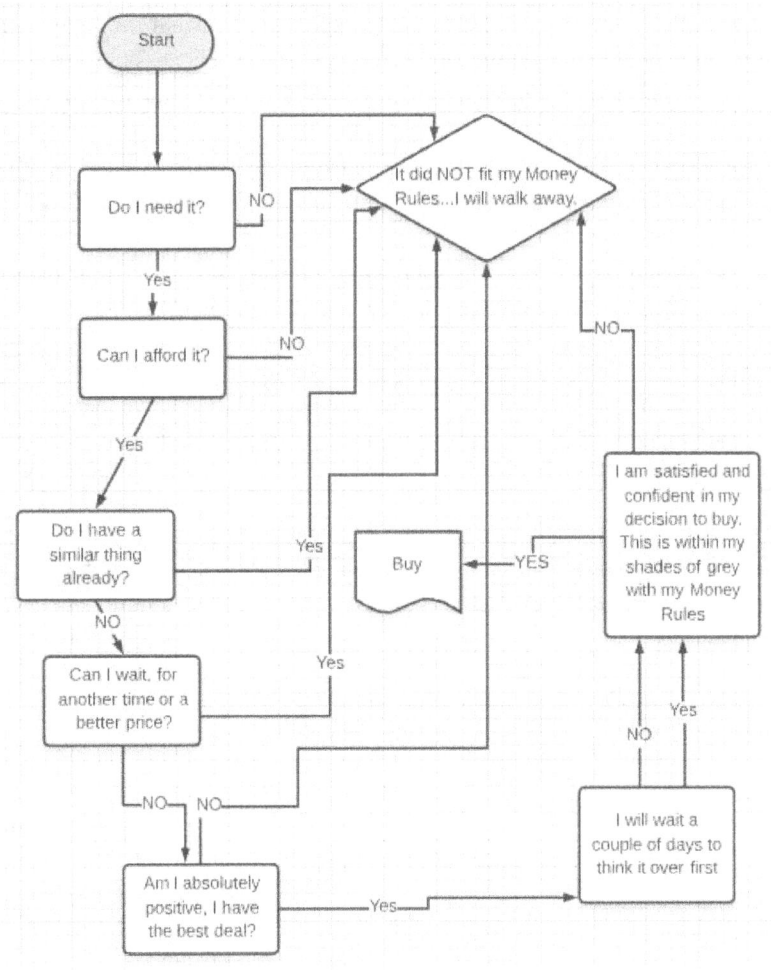

Mindset

Your mind is your biggest asset but can also be your biggest liability. The key is to play to your strengths, turn it into your greatest asset and reduce the liability time. I am no expert when it comes to mindset. I am very glad that I have experts in this field that I can talk to when needed. What I can say, though, is that your current mindset has gotten you to where you are today. It will not get you to where you want to be. That is the reality. As your knowledge of what is possible grows, your mindset will be more open to becoming what you need it to be. Whatever your current thinking is around money, wealth, finances and investing, be curious about new possibilities and know that what you want to achieve can happen when you open your mind to new ideas.

Lisa-Maree Botticelli, our go-to mindset expert in the wealth space and founder of http://purecreativitycoaching.com, has kindly shared a few pointers with us:

- Identify where you are sabotaging yourself and clear out the blocks that stop you from allowing in what you want to have in your life.

- Rewire your brain with a daily money mindset practice that creates new neural pathways, transforming old beliefs into new patterns for success.

- It's important to know what you want for your life so that you know what direction you want to take and then can set your mind to it.

- Using the power of the mind is the first step to your success.

- You must think high to rise. If you want to increase your financial abundance, setting your sights on higher goals requires higher ordered thinking and involves a change of mindset.

- Once you address those beliefs that aren't serving you well, clear out what holds you back and then align with those higher order goals to achieve the results you are looking for.

- The best way to transform your life is to back up belief with action.

- Follow successful actions with building momentum.

- Break your large steps down into small steps, define your actions and keep creating momentum.

- Stop settling for mediocrity. If you don't have a plan for your own life, you become someone else's plan.

- Refocus on your own dreams again by connecting with your authenticity and deeper truth.

- By changing the way you see things, you create a new way of being in the world.

- Changing your mindset is an inside job and leads to change on the outside.

- New opportunities will turn up to support you in having what you want for your life only when you create the necessary inner changes first.

- Reprogramming your mind will create a new way of seeing things, taking you to places previously unseen and unknown.

- By opening your mind to new ways of seeing and thinking, you also open the way to create abundance, prosperity and success.

- Your mind is connected to your being – Mind, Body, and Soul, it is all interlinked. When they are all working together, good stuff happens and flows. Easily and effortlessly.

Education, due diligence and review

Increasing your education and expanding your knowledge is the glue that keeps everything together. In our financial house checklist, reviews and education plans are the most important tasks, and should be set in stone in your diary and completed regularly.

Education is the difference between financial freedom and financial independence, so it is very important that you keep learning. Build your knowledge base so that when you are speaking with your accountant, advisor or wealth team, you can ask better questions. You can understand why they are suggesting a certain strategy. Taking advice without understanding it is a recipe for disaster and can quickly turn you from being financially free to having to go back to work at 55, 65 or older.

In Part Three of this book, where we lay out each step, every second step is around education, due diligence and reviewing what you have done and what you want to achieve for the next step. The Japanese have a saying: *kaizen*. It means "constant and never-ending improvement". This is needed in all areas of your life. We feel like a broken record, we repeat these things over and over. Without tracking your results, your investments, your spending, your weight loss, your..., how can you know you are making improvements? Without this foundation, all you have is a bunch of bricks that look like a house.

Due diligence is how you reduce your education costs. You pay for your education one way or another, and due diligence helps reduce your student fees.

Compounding doesn't just work with interest. It also works with your education. The more you read, watch, listen and experience in life, the more valuable (wealthy) you become, the more sought after (if that's what you want) you become, the more money you can charge and the more money you can invest. It all compounds and it all starts with you taking action. Investing the time to read this book and do the exercises contained within will help compound your wealth and set you on your way to achieving your dreams.

Jim Rohn states, "Formal education will make you a living, self-education will make you a fortune." We agree. We have more money from investing in ourselves than from anything we learnt at school.

Whatever you do, spend less than you make and invest in different assets – beginning with yourself

"But I don't have anything to invest." Boy, do we hear that a lot. BS, we say. You always have something to invest. In the next chapter, we share how, what and where you can find something to invest.

Biggest takeaways, actions required and notes

_____
_____
_____
_____
_____
_____
_____
_____
_____
_____
_____
_____
_____
_____
_____
_____
_____
_____
_____
_____
_____
_____
_____

Everybody has something to start investing with

There's a lot of people who believe that they don't have any assets to invest and yet, we all do. These are just the categories that we've come up with in terms of assets. You might have a few more as well.

- Time
- Money
- Knowledge/Skills
- Energy
- Connections
- Lazy Assets

Time

We believe that for those who say, "I don't have time to create wealth," or "I don't have time to get educated around wealth," it's just not a high priority for them. It's as simple as that. If you're going to spend time watching TV, then that's a bigger priority to you at that moment than building wealth, increasing your knowledge or researching investment strategies. Maybe you are avoiding what you know you need to do.

It sounds a little bit harsh, because we really like watching TV. We love watching movies. It's one of our hobbies and we enjoy it, but we do know that there have been times where we will just watch TV because we don't want to be doing something else. So, it comes down to priorities.

Money

Whenever we hear someone say they don't have any money to invest, we call BS on that too. We ALL have spare dollars. For some, it might just one dollar and for others, hundreds, but we all have some. What it boils down to is how you prioritise your current income and cash. The priority on how you can spend it is due to either choices you've made in the past or choices you need to make today and into the future.

We have always been able to find some money, even in the tightest of budgets. It's about tricking your mind, right? Turn around and say, "Hey, how could I find some extra money?" That money is either to invest to make more income, or even to speed up paying down your debts. Remember the Ninja tricks from earlier in this book?

Knowledge/Skills

We all have knowledge and skills as assets. We have picked these up at previous or current jobs, or from what we have studied or are studying. Most people don't realise that others want and need you to share your experiences, knowledge and skills. This can be made into an extra income stream or a full-time business – the choice is yours.

Energy

We all have high energy days and low energy days. Even over the course of one day, our energy can fluctuate. What do you spend your current energy on? Just getting by and hoping to pay off your debt some day? Or are you springing out of bed every day because you are living the life of your dreams?

Energy can be closely related to time as well, but some people have plenty of time and no energy, or they are spending their energy on things they truly don't want to. Toxic relationships, for example, can suck a lot of energy out of you.

Connections

Look to your connections and see who you can utilise (not use). It's about leverage. An exchange of value must occur to be a win-win-win. In most situations, we look for the three wins. The person using the product should win. As should the person who created it. The third win (which doesn't always need to be there) can be for the person promoting the product. This can also help people build other streams of income by being rewarded for sharing products or services they use and/or believe in. Seek out connections that can help you build an online business or start an offline business. You might only need a bit of coaching and their experience to get something started. People who are more successful than you are willing to share their skills and knowledge you if you're motivated.

Lazy Assets

What lazy assets do you have lying around? If you own a home, are you using the equity? Do you have a second car that you really don't need, or could do without for a while? Look to convert this into cash, ready to invest and/or pay down debt. You might even reduce time and energy by getting rid of these so-called assets (excluding the home at this point!).

Now you need to think about the level of involvement you want to put in to make these assets work for you (and potentially make these assets work harder). How much time do you want to spend getting involved in looking for properties, or buying shares, or trading shares, or trading forex? How much of your money do you want to be involved in that? Or how much of other people's money do you want involved? What knowledge and skills can you utilise to make more income? What energy will you put into it, and what connections could you utilise?

We are very well connected, and 99% of the time, if we don't know something, we know someone who knows it. It's a good way to be able to leverage your energy, your time, your skills and your money to get into it. So, what involvement are you willing to give?

What assets do you have to hand and what involvement level do you want? You can make it a number from one to 10 or a percentage, whatever the case may be. The more honest you are with yourself, the easier it will be for you to find which strategies will suit you and your priorities at a later time.

Assets in hand	**Involvement level**
Time	_____
Money	_____
Knowledge/skills	_____
Energy	_____
Connections	_____
Lazy Assets	_____

As you can see, we all have something that we can invest with. Most of us would rather find an excuse or blame others for their lack of money, assets, time, energy, etc. When will you take responsibility for your actions and/or inaction and do something about it? Like we said, if you need a hug, don't come to us. But if you want clarity on what you can do right now to improve your situation, then let's chat. Bring it on.

Case Studies – Our IAW members

When picking case studies to highlight, companies always choose the best of the best. And I get why. It shows what's possible. But somehow, whenever I've read them in the past, I've often thought two things: 1. Are they made up? (Yes, even I have thought that.) and 2. The results are exceptional, but can I achieve those if I decided to join that company?

The International Academy of Wealth could also highlight our best case studies:

- One member's $47k business loan wiped by a big four bank after implementing the strategies we gave him.
- Another reduced $55k worth of debt and made over $50k in returns within just four months of joining our community.
- Another purchased five properties in their first 12 months with us.
- Another added over $43.5k of passive income and is now *choosing* to work rather than *having* to.
- A single parent having no idea about household finances to being in full control of her money and saving her first $1k on her own. Going from relying on her husband for everything, to being an inspiration to her kids and single parents alike.
- A member got his finances sorted and now has a "van" account for his goal of buying a van and travel Australia. By implementing the strategies in the book, this will now be a reality. He is already one-third of the way to his goal.

The steps in this book work for all levels and all goals.

THE FUTURE OF INVESTING

Now we're starting to get into the guts of it. Before you read on, we just want to say again, thank you for making the decision to be here and spend the time increasing your knowledge. We saw this cool thing on Facebook the other day about how "you can either watch Netflix or you could have invested in Netflix". Over a certain period, the $10 monthly Netflix expense would have cost you about $600. If you had invested that $600 into Netflix when it started, it would have been worth $40,000 today.

We all could be doing something else, so we are grateful you are here and we are hoping that you're really getting to understand that the world has changed, and that you've made the decision to learn everything about it.

If you truly understand the future of investing, you'll see that you'll be able to make better and, we believe, more profitable decisions to get to that point where you're financially independent.

Let's look at the Five Cs of the Future of Investing. We want you to grab a pen and paper and get into this right now.

Control

We really believe that, moving forward, you need to have more control over your investing and your investment education than ever before.

Control over your money, absolutely – and control over who you give it to and over the due diligence that you do. If you think that, with all your investments moving forward, you'll have complete control of your money, it's not going to happen. However, you want to control who you give it to and that's done via the due diligence that you conduct on an investment opportunity.

We've noticed lately that some of the biggest scams we've seen online involve people who want you to send them money so they can trade for you or whatever. For a very high percentage of those "opportunities", the money will not come back. That's a stat from personal experience. We do have a couple of investment strategies where we send the money on to somebody and they trade with it. We don't compound those opportunities as quickly as we do with other opportunities, because what we do is get that capital back as fast as possible and leave the profits in. That is one way that you can control it. A lot of the opportunities that we look at, the money sits in your account (e.g. a forex or share trading account) and it gets traded for you. You sign a document to state that the trader you have chosen can trade your account on your behalf.

Control your environment. We believe that that your environment is going to control what your future looks like, and you have full control of your environment. You need to look at it and ask, "How tidy is my workspace?" and "Who am I hanging around with?" You want to make sure that it's where you want to be. It's something that we are getting better at ourselves, choosing who we hang out with and the types of conversations that we have.

There's nothing wrong with having different types of conversations. Sometimes we just want to talk about the weather. Sometimes we just want to talk about rugby or sports or whatever. But at other times, if your conversations are about how you can do better in the world or how you can help other people, then there's that old saying, "the more people you help get what they want, the more likely it is that you'll get what you want". The key to that is very control of your environment and who you hang out with.

Control your education. We can't stress that enough. We believe that what's getting taught in our schools is just utterly ridiculous. A lot of it isn't even going to help people in life, and it's frustrating. We would love to see you control your education. If you're no longer in school, then you have 100% control of your education, and you get to decide who and what you listen to. Remember how we said you'll have to decide? You need to look at it and ask, "What decision am I going to make today around my wealth education? Am I going to listen to Mark or Billie and get some more education from them, their community and team of experts? Or am I going to just completely ignore all this and keep listening to what the system is telling us to do?"

Control your investments. Look at what you're investing in and see if it's going to get you to your End Game. It's key for you to understand. Will those property investments allow you to become financially independent sooner or is that a long-term opportunity and you'll need some other types of investments to speed it all up?

Connect

We believe you need to connect with like-minded people and that's what we love about the International Academy of Wealth, that it's an application process. We want to hang around with and connect with like-minded people. We've seen programs out there in the past where, as long as you've got a credit card and a pulse, you're in. That's not the case with us. It sounds like a little plug to "The Academy", but we're really proud of the fact that that's what we've done – connect with like-minded people.

Connect with different people outside your circle. This is a little bit harsh, but it's true. There's a good chance that they could be why you are not where you want to be. We love going back to our old hometowns and hanging out with people from our past, but it's not the people that we hang out with 80%, 90% or 95% of the time. We want to hang out with like-minded people, people who want to do good in the world.

> *"Knowing the limits of your circle of competence is more important than being brilliant and thinking your circle of competence includes every investment strategy."*
> *– Warren Buffet*

Connect with people who are doing or have done what you want to do. That's key. We never want to be smartest or wealthiest person in the room. How much knowledge and learning can we get from all the other people in the room if we already know and have more than everyone else? Not much. That's what it's about. We want to connect with and be around people who are doing what we want to do and/or have already done it.

Community

Wealth is not just about the money. Money helps, without a doubt. But it's about the wealth of experiences, the wealth of knowledge, the wealth of love, the wealth of friendships. That, to us, is our truth. We believe that we're the wealthiest people in the world because we've got the love of each other, the love of our family, the love of our friends. We've got respect and we appreciate and are grateful for everything we have.

These photos below are of a couple of experiences we've had that will be with us forever – being welcomed to the land by the local Maori tribe in New Zealand and our base camp in Hawaii. Both these experiences were with the International Academy of Wealth community.

These memories will last a lifetime. They were incredible experiences and that is what life is about. We also hang around with other communities that are going to educate us as well. Perhaps you should too. We love doing what we do, and we're passionate about it. It's exciting to be a part of so many people's wealth creation journeys.

Collaborate

We can't stress enough how important this is, and we love that we get to collaborate with other like-minded people and experts in different fields. We collaborate with experts in the fields of due diligence, share trading software, language, and even with a real-life samurai. It's fantastic. They say it takes about 10,000 hours of education to be an expert.

What you can do, with collaboration, is get someone else to do those 10,000 hours while you keep doing what you're doing. That's what we love about being part of a community that understands this. 30 years of information is shared every single month within the International Academy of Wealth because of the research everyone does collaboratively. This helps you speed up your learning and creates win-win-win opportunities.

Compound

We believe the future of investments has to have this component of compounding to really accelerate your wealth. Albert Einstein said, *"Compound interest is the eighth wonder of the world. He who understands it, earns it ... he who doesn't ... pays it."* We are going to say that one more time. **"He who understands it, earns it ... he who doesn't ... pays it."**

Here is an example. This credit card is $38,273 in debt. If all they did was make the minimum repayment of $765, it would take 141 years to pay off, and rack up total interest charges of $292,825. Almost $293k and 141 years to pay off! Do you think the banks understand what compound interest is and why they love it when you only make the minimum repayments?

Opening balance at 21 Nov	$37,769.95
New transactions and charges	$1,264.17
Payments/refunds	-$761.00
Closing balance at 20 Dec	$38,273.12
Next statement period	21 Dec 2018 - 18 Jan 2019

Total amount owing	$38,273.12
Minimum payment	$765.00
Payment due by	14 Jan 2019

Your account is overlimit.
Please pay the overlimt amount of $273.12 immediately to ensure you can continue transacting on your account.

Minimum Repayment Warning: If you make only the minimum payment each month, you will pay more interest and it will take you longer to pay off your balance. For example:

If you make no additional charges using this card and each month you pay...	You will pay off the Closing Balance shown on this statement in about...	And you will end up paying estimated total interest charges of...
Only the minimum payment	141 years, 1 month	$292,825.74
$1,971.20	2 years	$9,035.78, a saving of $283,789.96

Now, let's look at the other side. Take $50,000 and invest it in an opportunity that uses roughly the same income rates as the credit cards charge. We're comparing apples with apples. And we do have opportunities that pay around that 15% per annum. One particular investment has paid 15% per annum for the last 16 years, like clockwork.

After just 10 years, you would have made $240,000. If you took another 10 years, it would be worth $526k. Another five years, you've got $1.1 million. At 25 years, your $50k, by compounding it, has turned into $2.5 million.

It doesn't matter how old you are or how much you currently have in your portfolio. If you understand the power of compounding interest, you will earn it. If you don't, you will pay it. Do you want to understand it? The banks really do understand the power of compounding interest.

Account Value	
$50,000.00	$384,933.94
$58,500.00	$450,372.71
$68,445.00	$526,936.07
$80,080.65	$616,515.21
$93,694.36	$721,322.79
$109,622.40	$843,947.66
$128,258.21	$987,418.77
$150,062.11	$1,155,279.96
$175,572.66	$1,351,677.55
$205,420.42	$1,581,462.73
$240,341.42	$1,850,311.40
$281,199.46	$2,164,864.34
$329,009.37	$2,532,891.28

They want you to be enslaved for 141 years, rather than being free in 5, 10, 20, 25 years. That's what we really want you to understand – the power of compounding. **He who understands it, earns it, he who doesn't, pays it.**

Bonus Section – Opportunities

We weren't going to add this section in. However, we thought, "If we are truly going to give a complete do-it-yourself road map, then there needs to be something in here about our opinion on which types of opportunities or asset sectors are worth doing due diligence on." So here it is – our thoughts on where you could spend some time researching and, if it fits your Money Rules, investing in.

NOTE: These are just what we think are worth looking into, nothing more. We are not recommending, in any way, that you should go out and invest your money in ANY investment within the below sectors.

AI

Artificial intelligence (AI) is an exciting area to look into. You can research how the technology is playing out in a number of areas – from smarter computers, through to share trading, FX trading, etc.

Blockchain

We've lumped blockchain and cryptocurrency under one sector. Start with a basic understanding of what blockchain is and how it is impacting a lot of different industries. If you understand the power of blockchain you will get excited. Cryptocurrency is also worth spending time on. Look at it from an asset perspective, rather than an industry. Look to buy and hold, trade and short crypto. This is a book in its own right, so we'll leave it there. People who know me are thinking that I must be sick or something, as it has taken 100-odd pages for us to finally mention blockchain and crypto.

Cannabis

Love it or hate it, cannabis is a massive, newly legal market that is set to boom in the next five years or more. Obviously, if you have strong feelings against cannabis, then don't waste your time researching this market. If you do have an interest, then you will love what is happening in this space. From, growing and financing, to "corner stores" and edibles, the market is massive.

Diamonds

Diamonds are girl's best friend, as they say. They can also be an investor's as well. We are not talking local jeweller quality. You need to find investment-quality diamonds to have any chance of making money in this asset class. We may know some people who can help here.

EAs and social trading

Expert advisors (EAs) are pieces of software that trade for you, based on algorithms. Social trading is when you follow other traders who are successful. They will provide you with signals for when to buy and sell. We like EAs and another route called copy trading. Copy trading is just that. When the trader trades, your account trades. You don't need to know how to trade. We at the Academy have some exciting opportunities in this space, in FX, share trading and options. You can either copy trade, social trade or have an EA trade for you.

Gold and Silver

Can be an insurance against a global financial meltdown. It's a long-term play and worth investigating, should it meet your Money Rules.

Internet of Things

Incredible space and you can get lost in several rabbit holes when going down this path. Think of everything being connected – that is what this space is about.

Sustainable anything

Why waste and/or kill the planet if we don't have to? Solar, wind and other viable energy sources. Better farming and production. We will also add in this section smart cities, although this could be a sector by itself.

Services for baby boomers

Ah, our mates, the baby boomers. They did everything that was fun to excess then made it illegal. As the biggest population on the planet, their need for services is increasing. From spending their children's inheritance (good on them, we say), to high quality travel, to medical aid devices. Anything that makes their life easier and prolongs it.

Other sectors you could look into are:
- 3D printing
- Health tech
- Mobile and social internet
- Big data
- Online gaming and gambling
- Nanotechnology
- Automation
- Driverless vehicles
- Robots.

There are plenty of things you can research and make incredible profits from. Just remember your Money Rules. Another deal will always come along. Does it have the Five Cs of the Future of Investing?

This chapter can also help guide you with the next section – adding an income stream. We'll show you the steps you can take to invest in an income stream or asset. It is a process that can be repeated over and over.

ADDING ANOTHER INCOME STREAM

People tend to get caught up thinking that adding another income stream is difficult. But that couldn't be further from the truth. Below is the step-by-step process that you can use time and time again to add an asset or income stream and become financially independent.

Let's run through each step now.

1. Why?

Why do you want to add an income stream? It sounds like a crazy question. However, you need to know why. Giving it a purpose will make it easier to decide what type of income stream, and what type of asset to invest in to create the income stream.

Is it to:
- reduce debt?
- increase net investable income?
- increase net investable capital?
- reduce your active income hours?
- increase passive income?
- increase laptop income?

What are you prepared to sacrifice to achieve the goal of adding an income stream? We are not talking about going against your values or doing something illegal. We are talking about what you do with your spare time. Will you watch TV or learn to create more money?

2. Money Rules.

Does adding another one, two, or even three income streams fit with your Money Rules? Right now, you may be better off increasing a current one than adding a new income stream. That is why you need to ask this question. If it is a no, then you have saved a bunch of time. If it is a yes, continue to 3.

3. Research
Here's what you need to research to make sure you know exactly what you're getting into:

4. Type of income stream.
Where in the formula will the income stream place? AI or PI or LTI? Will you get a second job, or investigate social trading or bot trading? Will you increase or start your laptop income?

5. From where?
What assets on hand will you use to add an income stream? Time, money, knowledge/skills, energy, connections or lazy assets?

6. Decisions
Decide which opportunity you will investigate, e.g. property shares, business, trading, etc. Do they have the Five Cs that the Future of Investing must have?

7. Money Rules
Does this opportunity fit your Money Rules? If no, find another. If yes, move to the next step.

8. Due diligence
DD / DYOR (do your own research) is the number one reason you will succeed or fail in investing.

9. Action plan
Map out the steps you need to take, and the timing needed for you to get this new income stream in place. What education gaps do you have that may prevent you from taking action? Who do you need on your team?

10. Rinse and repeat

Once you have the income stream or have purchased the asset, go back to step 1 and start again to add another asset and/or income stream.

This process eliminates the guesswork and will reduce risk significantly. **IT DOES NOT ELIMINATE RISK.** Many a guru will tell you to do due diligence, and yet have no idea how to do it themselves. Inside the Academy, we have our own DD lab. We have laid out the process, making it easier for you to understand DD and the process you need to follow, and reducing the risk as much as possible.

Biggest takeaways, actions required and notes

PART THREE – THE ULTIMATE WEALTH PLAN AND PUTTING IT ALL TOGETHER

"Wealthy people maximize investments (in themselves and in business) while minimizing expenses. while the poor do the opposite. Being poor is not so much an income but a mindset and the results of the habits that come from that mindset."
– Warren Buffet

"The best investment for one year is to grow grains; the best investment for ten years is to grow trees; the best investment for a lifetime is to educate people. What you gain from one year's growth will be grains; what you gain

from ten years' growth will be trees; what you gain from a hundred years' growth will be people."
– Guan Zhong

Getting to your destination is easier when you know where you are going, what equipment you need to get there and have any foreseeable hazards laid out before you leave. We have shared some of the hazards that we foresee coming in earlier chapters. You now know what you need to do to prepare for the trip ahead. Imagine having a blueprint of how to get to where you want to be. Having each step laid out with the tools you will need will not only help you arrive safely but will accelerate and reduce the time it takes. Everybody's wealth journey is unique, yet the steps you need to take are pretty much the same. Some steps are interchangeable with others. Some you can skip, while others you will need to stay a bit longer in.

Think of each step as a country town. Sometimes we need to pull over and get some petrol and supplies, while with other towns we can stay on the road and keep going. With research, you can make a full list of every town and what it can do for you – what tools and supplies they can give you. If you don't need anything, then you can drive on to the next town. By following these steps, your journey will be more like staying on the motorway and only stopping for short breaks along the way.

95% of people reading this book will need to call into "Wake-the-F$%&-Upsville", before heading into "Admit-You-Need-Helptown". That's OK. We have been there and "visited" that. In fact, for a number of years we stayed at "Denial Hotel" and drank at the "Bury Your Heads in the Sand Bar".

In Part Three, we outline each step and what you need to do in detail. In every step, there are different levels or ways that you can complete it and move forward.

The fastest way to gain control and build wealth is increase your income and reduce your expenses. This is also the fastest way to becoming financially free.

When looking at our own experiences in becoming financially independent, there is one way that stands out as the fastest. That way is to build a business. Not everyone is cut out to be a business owner or entrepreneur, despite what some of the gurus on stage who want you to buy their stuff will say. Nor is everyone destined to be an educated investor. Most, like I said before, won't do anything with this information. Those that do will have a better chance of being financially independent.

We are now 100% unemployable. I have been self-employed now since I was about 20. There have been a couple of stints back in "Jobland". At the last one, they made me turn up by 8:30am and would not let me leave until 5:30pm. Please understand that we believe being an employee is perfectly fine – but only if that is what you feel is best for you, your family and your best path to create financial independence. Your life, your way, remember.

In another of our books, 'Winning the Wealth Game in Business', we go into more detail, so we won't bore you here. What we will share is the four things wealthy entrepreneurs do better than non-wealthy business owners:

1. **Invest in themselves.** They will see that joining the International Academy of Wealth, for example, is an investment in their wealth education and not an expense.
2. **Develop people.** Successful entrepreneurs build leaders and develop their people, their team.
3. **Develop turnkey systems.** They ensure that as they grow the business, each step is turned into a system that anyone can follow (think McDonald's).
4. **Duplicate what works.** They find what works and duplicate it. No matter how boring it is – if it works, then don't fix it, duplicate it.

A business done right can allow you to work your own hours, work where you want and with whom you want to.

WHAT IT TAKES TO BE WEALTHY

Some parts of this section we have already said, multiple times. Other parts will be new to this book. We felt that it was important to share our thoughts one last time before you start to learn the steps. At the end of the day, wealth can be achieved by anyone willing to accept that they do not know everything, and that others may know what they need. Not everyone is out to scam you. Some of us just want to share with you what has worked for us and our community. If you are open-minded and curious about what is possible, then you have a chance to be wealthy.

Here are some other tips that we believe will make your journey to financial independence easier:

Learn to sell

By far, the best skill you can learn is to sell. Learning to sell a product, a service, or your skills and knowledge will be the most profitable skill and it will change your life. Our friends joke that I'm punching above my weight with Billie as my wife. I tend to agree, and I wake up every day and think, "What do I need to do today to ensure she sees the value in me staying around?" Maybe I'm just a great salesman. My first direct sales role was at the bank. However, the one that taught me that I will be rewarded if I just get off my backside and work a bit harder than the next person was in real estate. The bank gave everyone a pay rise, no matter how hard each person worked. In real estate, if we didn't sell, we didn't eat. The first year, we were on a retainer plus commission. We earned $32k. The next year, we were on commission only and we earned $132k. A bit of motivation goes a long way. Learn to sell. It will help you in all areas of life, from romance to finance.

Learn to lead

In 1936, Dale Carnegie wrote, "15% of one's financial success is due to one's technical abilities and the other 85% is due to skill in human engineering – to personality and the ability to lead people". We believe that learning to lead will also help you build long term financial independence.

Reduce outgoings
Start getting your expenses under control and within your means.

Increase income streams
No longer can you rely on one income stream per person, let alone per household. The wealthy have multiple streams – learn from that.

Change of mindset
You are where you are right now due to your current mindset. To get to where you want to be will require you to change your mindset.

Change of habits
As your mindset is changed, so will your habits – both the ones that have held you back as well as the new ones that will form to help you achieve all that you want.

Who do you listen to?
If you are listening to friends, family, work colleagues or know-it-alls at the BBQ, ignore their well-meaning advice – unless they have achieved what you want to achieve. Start listening to successful people who want to help others.

Don't do it alone
When you start to move outside your comfort zone, the last thing you want to be is alone. That's why we developed the International Academy of Wealth, so that like-minded people don't have to take this journey alone.

Learn from the mistakes of others
You pay for your education one way or another. Save some dollars and learn from the mistakes of others. We share the good, the great and the ugly, in the hope that you don't have to go down that path. Our mistakes have cost us millions, and yet here we are, still doing what we love. No one likes to lose a million dollars, yet everyone would like to have a million dollars to lose.

Understand the rules

The wealthy play with different rules. These rules are available to everyone. You need to know which ones will benefit you now and into the future.

Winter is coming

We love the 'Game of Thrones' series, both the books and the TV show. "Winter is coming", to us, sums up what is ahead regarding the world economy, the local economy and investing in general. Winter is coming and those that are prepared for it now will not only survive the fallout but thrive. We are happy to profit from other people's greed, stupidity and lack of drive. It is *not* about preying on people's misfortunes – it's about ensuring a win-win-win for everyone, where possible.

Have fun

Even in the darkest of days, when we knew the money had been taken or when the employee had screwed us big time, we still laughed and had fun. Life is too short not to.

Enjoy the journey

No one gets out alive and you can't take it with you. Smell the roses, love, sing, be a good human being and enjoy the journey. The steps coming up will allow you to choose how you enjoy the journey, whether on foot or by plane. Now, someone right now is thinking "I like to walk". Who doesn't? But there's a difference between choosing to walk and having to.

PUTTING IT ALL TOGETHER –
THE ULTIMATE WEALTH ACCELERATION PLAN

"I insist on a lot of time being spent, almost every day, to just sit and think. That is very uncommon in American business. I read and think. So I do more reading and thinking, and make less impulse decisions than most people in business."
– *Warren Buffett*

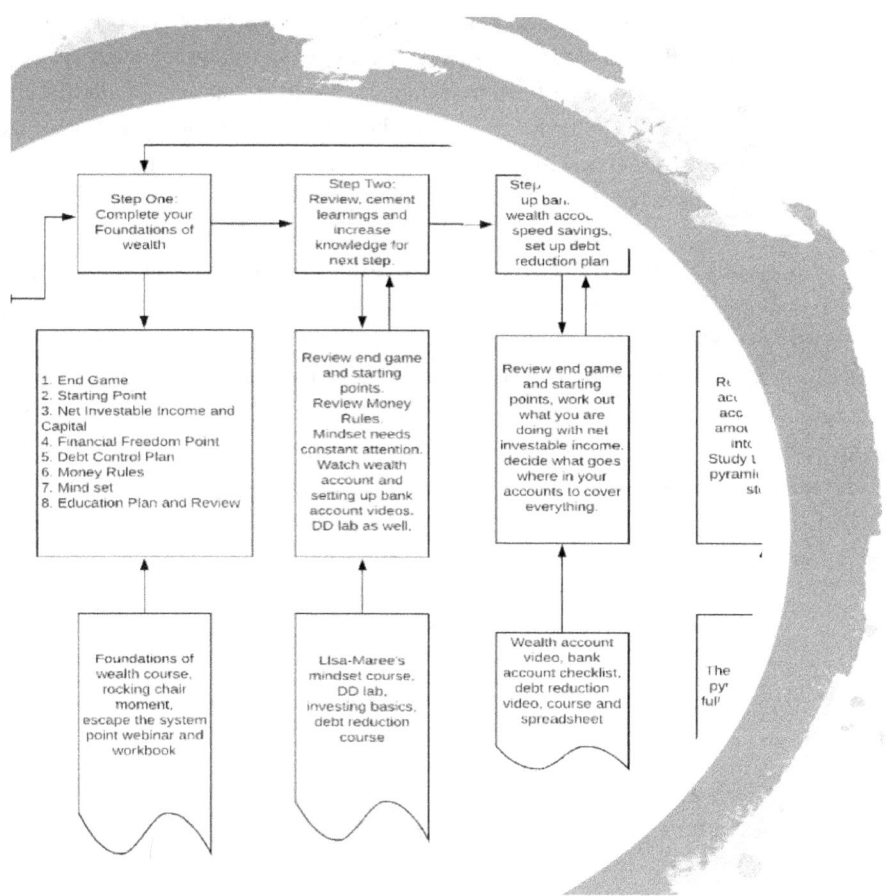

This diagram is a sneak peek at the Ultimate Wealth Acceleration Program. The steps to follow are simple to take, but you do have to put them into action. You can make them work for you. For example, you might find you prefer to work with only two or three bank accounts. Or you might want one bank account for every goal. This is where you start to build your own financial independence formula, using the Ultimate Wealth Acceleration Plan. We have our wealth account set up in a company trust structure. You may end up using a company, or just have everything in your own names. As long as it works for you and your family, it doesn't matter how you're set up. You might have less than 10 Money Rules, or you might have 100. You might keep records to the cent or maybe being within a hundred bucks will do.

Keep it simple and it will work better for you. While we have covered all the steps that we believe you need to take, some can be skipped if not needed – you can easily come back to those steps. Debt is a great example. If you have consumer debt, look to reduce it as fast as you can. Does it mean you should not invest until you have cleared it completely? No. You can invest before wiping out the debt, but you should check in with your Money Rules. Should you never borrow money? No. Using leverage (borrowing) can be a great way to accelerate your wealth. Done correctly, that is. What do your Money Rules say?

Some steps you CANNOT skip, however. Due diligence, reviews and education are 100% non-negotiable. Look to *kaizen* everything you do. Simplify everything. Systemise everything. Understand everything that is going on – but you do not have to do everything. You can hire accountants, financial planners, mortgage brokers, wealth education experts, trading experts, property experts. You just need to understand the why, what, how and when of the strategy you are adding to your financial independence formula.

- What goal will this strategy help me achieve?
- When should I deploy it?
- How should I deploy it?
- Who should help me?
- What Money Rules cover my decision?

After each attacking step, there will always be a defensive step or two. The starting few steps are very much in defence. Laying the foundations and building your financial house are key to keeping your wealth. We have always said, "Making money is easy, keeping it is the trick." That is why the emphasis is 80% on defence and 20% on attack. When your defences are strong, then it can be the other way around with 80% attack and 20% defence. Or 50/50, 60/40. You will know what is best for you

They say it takes 10,000 hours to become an expert. You will need to build up to 7-10 hours per week of financial education if you are going to become an expert in your financial independence. Remember, you do not need to know everything. You do need to know everything about your finances. There is no better person to direct your wealth team than you. Seek responsibility over advice. Yes, you can seek advice, but look to ask better questions from your advisors so you get better answers.

Let's get this party started.

> *"Making money is easy, keeping it is the trick."*
> – Mark & Billie Robinson

Preparation

Preparation is simple.

Be open-minded. Be curious. Be honest with yourself. Do you truly want financial independence? It is OK if you don't. Maybe you just want to be better than you are right now. It will save you time if you decide that right now. If so, go see a financial planner or use one that understands what we do.

Re-read this book. Get a good understanding of what we are about. Write notes all over it. Jess, our community book editor, will NOT be happy I said this!

Complete the exercises contained within the book. This will speed up some of the steps coming up and cement the learnings as well.

Look to build up to 7-10 hours a week of financial education.

Collaborate with like-minded people. Join our open Facebook group: https://www.facebook.com/groups/learngrowacceleratewealth/

Set time aside each day or week to get these steps completed. If it's not in your diary, then it's not a priority and it simply won't happen.

Consistent steps will win the race.

Enjoy the journey.

Step 1: The Foundations of Wealth

In Part Two of this book, you have all the steps you need to complete the foundations of wealth. Each foundation connects with the others. They intertwine to help you build solid foundations for your financial house. If you do not know what your End Game looks like – i.e. what your income, expenses and net worth will be when you are financially free – then how can you plan what you need to do to achieve financial freedom, and then financial independence? Same goes with Money Rules and mindset. If you keep the same mindset and Money Rules that got you to where you are today, there's a good chance you will not be able to get to where you want to be. Mindset and Money Rules will constantly be changing as your wealth grows.

Go through each step, review, tweak and complete.
1. End Game
2. Starting point
3. Net investable income and capital
4. Financial freedom point
5. Debt control plan
6. Money Rules
7. Mindset
8. Financial House
9. Education plan and review

The above you can do yourself. If you would like to learn about our Foundations of Wealth course, see the back of the book for more information on how we can help accelerate your wealth and guide you.

Step 2: Review, Cement and Increase

From Step 1, you would have started creating an action plan. Maybe you need more help with your mindset. Or you need help with setting your Money Rules. Understandable, as some of this is completely new to you. In Step 2, you review your action/education plan and what you have completed in the foundations of wealth. From there, you take action. Start thinking along the lines of who you need in your wealth team to make this a reality. What news channels, newsletters or social media do you need to add or cut out of your life to change your mindset? By doing this, you can improve on what you have or completely change today. This is where we start to feel uncomfortable. You might even start (OK, there is no might) to have friends you no longer want to hang with as they are part of your problem. Been there, done that. You start to hunt out different conversations.

In this step, look to:
- Review your foundations and make adjustments where needed.
- Write down what you learnt from completing your foundations of wealth. Take your time. Remember to find a quiet place with no distractions. It is the best way to cement the learnings.
- Write down your education plan. What do you need to do to increase your knowledge of what you just learnt and what do you need to learn for the next step?
- Review the next step to get ready.

Book a call with us if you need some help. (Contact details are at the back of the book.)

Step 3: Banking, Debt Control Plan and Speed Savings

This step is so simple, and yet by far one of the most effective. In fact, setting up our wealth account and bank accounts properly and implementing our debt management plan was a large part of how we became financially independent. Without this step, we would not have accelerated our investing, our savings, or reduced our debt faster than the banks wanted us to.

In this step:
- Set up your wealth account and create an automatic payment to it each pay day for a chosen amount.
- Set up your bank accounts to suit your circumstances: e.g. everyday account, bills account, don't ask account, etc.
- Implement your debt management plan. This may include cutting up credit cards, combining debts into one, and setting up automatic payments so you don't focus on the debts.
- If need be, watch our videos on setting up an effective wealth account and banking system.
- Set up the speed savings strategy that fits your Money Rules, if any.

NOTE: For extra security, have your banking away from your lending. Most banks have what they call an 'all money' clause within your mortgage contract. Simply put, they can take any cash you have and use it to pay down debt if they want to. Even if they don't, why take the chance?

Step 4: Review, Cement and Increase.

You can see the pattern, right? Every second step is a review, cement and increase. Review what you have done, cement the learnings and increase your knowledge – ready for the next step. Steps 1-4 are very much entrenched in defence. It's what's needed right now. Most of you have been playing too much attack and, worse, the wrong type of attack. Impulse buying and spending money whenever you want is not attack. These steps do not need to take weeks, days or hours. They can be done quickly once you have your systems in place.

In this step:
- Review your banking plan and debt management plan.
- Review your foundations, ensuring you are on track.
- Check in with your mindset.
- Review your action and education plan. What is missing? What can you take off or add?
- Book a call with us, if needed, so we can help.

Step 5: Complete the Ultimate Wealth Plan Spreadsheet

It does not have to be our spreadsheet that you complete. It can be your own. As we keep saying, this journey is yours – build it your way.

If using your own, ensure it has the following:
- future income and expenses,
- future assets and liabilities,
- current income and expenses,
- current assets and liabilities.

Check out ours here: http://www.theinternationalacademyofwealth.com/uwps to see if it would work better for you. The UWPS allows you to keep what you need to build, track and accelerate your wealth in one place. It also allows you to keep it offline for added security.

In this step:
- Transfer your End Game and starting point information into the UWPS.
- Transfer your Money Rules into the UWP.
- Watch the "how to" videos to maximise the use of the UWPS.
- Add a password to the UWPS to protect it.
- Have different names for your investments so only you and your family know where everything is.
- Use the compounding calculator and scenario page to get used to those features (or your own). It is important to know these for the next step.

Step 6: Review, Cement and Increase

Like the jab-jab-cross is a great defensive move in boxing, so is review, cement and increase. These steps will take less time as you get used to doing them. They will, however, always be important. Skipping these will be the difference between being financially free and broke. If you are not into boxing, think cuddle, cuddle kiss.

In this step:
- Review your foundations and make adjustments where needed.
- Review your banking plan and debt reduction plan.
- Review your foundations, ensuring you are on track
- Check in with your mindset.
- Review your action and education plan. What is missing? What can you take off or add?
- Review your UWPS.
- Book a call with us, if needed, so we can help.

Step 7: Add an Income or Asset

"Finally!" we can hear you say. We get it. Defence can be boring. But, without good defence, your attack has to win 100% of the time. In my experience, that never happens. It is why we focus on the defence plan first, and then the attack. Get this right and your attack can have a couple of losing moves, but you will still win the game.

Here is the process to add an income stream or asset:
1. Why
2. Money Rules
3. Type of income
4. From where
5. Decide which one
6. Money Rules
7. Due diligence
8. Action plan
9. Rinse and repeat.

Go back and review any chapters you might need a refresher on to complete this step.

Step 8: Rinse and Repeat

Step 8 is a "rinse and repeat". Look at what worked for you and what didn't work. What areas do you need help in? Repeat Step 7 as often as you can. Build up the compounding effect of multiple assets and income streams to become financially free. Continuing wealth education will make you financially independent.

As your wealth grows, advanced strategies may be required and may include:
- Stronger asset protection planning.
- Estate planning.
- Tax planning.
- Global investing.
- Storing gold, silver, diamonds offshore.
- Structures such as companies, trusts, self-managed super funds (self-directed IRAs).
- Dual citizenship.
- Offshore structures and investing.

If the above advanced strategies pique your interest and are what you might be needing, then we definitely need to chat.

Step 9: What's next?

This book and the steps outlined within it can be used as your guide to "do it yourself".

People often want to learn to fish and then will just go out and fish. However, there are people who want to learn more about fishing and, when they take their first cast, they are keen to have an experienced fishing guide next to them. Others want to hang with other fishing enthusiasts while learning to fish, and others still just want the fish. The fishing analogy sums up the next steps nicely.

You can take this book and do it yourself. Or if you need more guidance in the different areas of financial education such as debt management, foundations of wealth, financial house and you want to be with a like-minded community, we have outlined on the next few pages on how you can receive that help.

Those that are "do it yourself" people, you can duplicate this for you and your family. You can share it with your wealth team, accountants, financial planners. The choice is yours. Most advisors will not get what this system is all about, as it gives you full control of what you do and not them. They can't hide behind complex statements of advice that none of their clients read fully. This system will arm you with better questions when dealing with advisors, accountant, brokers, etc. The world of investing is so complex, and it doesn't have to be.

In the last few years as a licensed advisor, I knew that we could not give advice in every area that our clients required. With the way the system is now, you will need an advisor for your insurances, an advisor for your super, an advisor for your investments, an advisor for your company tax and an advisor for your personal tax. All of them costing thousands of dollars per year.

By following the steps provided, you can reduce the number of advisors, or at least reduce the amount of advice required. **WE ARE NOT SAYING YOU DON'T NEED ADVICE.** We are asking you to take responsibility for your own wealth and become educated on what you need, not what the system tells you that you need. Less than 5%

of advisors in Australia are truly independent. They are hard to find. Most cannot give advice on property, business, currency trading, social trading, cryptocurrency, etc. It is our belief that you should be able to go to an advisor and pay for advice. If the advisor is not licensed to sell (yes, sell) you that product, then they cannot give advice under the current system. Why is that, do you think?

This is why becoming educated in what is out there gives the control back to you. If, after going through the above steps and finding out the types of investment strategies that are now available to you, you decide that the current system is where you want to be, then we have still done our job. We have given you the tools and information to make a choice – a choice that is based on more information than you had before. No matter what you decide to do, you made the decision and it will be the right one for you. If, on the other hand, you are excited to know there is light at the end of the tunnel, a community out there that can support you on your journey, and that there are other options out there than the ones we have been taught, then we have a solution for you.

Wanting to live life on purpose and improving your financial position can be a lonely road to travel, but it doesn't have to be. It is why we created the International Academy of Wealth – a community full of like-minded people who look to help people up, not hold them down. We celebrate the wins and group together when needed. We share and collaborate to speed up your education. We laugh, have fun and make the journey to financial independence an amazing one.

Our community get-togethers are always the highlight of our calendars. We have trusted experts in different areas of wealth available when the community needs them. The education that is provided is always ahead of the masses. There are live events and weekly webinars. Our membership site also has over four years of wealth education, and it continues to grow every week.

We also understand people are at different stages in their financial education journey. This is why we have different entry levels to the Academy, from do-it-yourself courses and guides right up to lifetime membership. Over the next few pages, explore which step is right for you. Every option comes with our 100% money-back guarantee. We do not want to keep any money from people who choose not to see and extract the value we provide. If you are curious about how we can work together, check them out.

We look forward to being of service to those that are ready to find the soul purpose of wealth, so that you can free your soul and live life on purpose.

Mark & Billie Robinson

NEXT STEPS

Debt Management Plan module

By completing this course, you will be able to:
- Identify which debt is best to pay off first.
- Work out how much in interest and fees you will save by paying down your debt the right way.
- Develop a debt reduction plan that you can stick to, including building your investing strategies and enjoying life with less stress.
- Develop a spending plan that allows you to live for today and plan for tomorrow.
- Understand how to negotiate your current debt and potentially save years and thousands of dollars.
- Become confident in your financial affairs and know that there is light at the end of the tunnel.

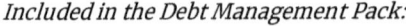

Included in the Debt Management Pack:
- Debt reduction calculator and videos on how to use it,
- DIY debt negotiation package including forms and how-to video series,
- Free private and confidential consult with Greg Watson – our debt and financial expert,
- Access to like-minded Facebook community group,
- Lifetime updates,
- Monefly wealth tracking tool and how-to-use video series,
- Speed savings series – a complete step-by-step process to setting up the three speed savings ideas,
- Calculators, tools, templates and how-to videos on the best way to utilise the program,
- Plus, a bunch of bonuses as well. Check the website for more information.

Join us at
www.TheInternationalAcademyOfWealth.com/DebtPlan

Foundations of Wealth program

By completing this program, you will be able to:

- Develop solid financial foundations to help you build, grow and accelerate your wealth.
- Decide what you are going to build your financial house with, to withstand any threat to your assets and lifestyle.
- Have a better understanding of your End Game financial position.
- Know in detail your starting point and net investable income.
- Build your own wealth education action plan.
- Develop healthy money habits.
- Work out your financial freedom point.

Foundations of wealth course includes:
- 9 modules to guide you, step by step, to build your foundations of wealth,
- Videos, checklists, workbooks to help you build solid foundations,
- Access to a like-minded Facebook group to accelerate your education,
- Escape the system point workbook,
- Free, private and confidential foundations of wealth chat with Mark Robinson – CEO and founder of the International Academy of Wealth,
- Plus: a bunch of other bonuses as well. Check the website for more information.

Join us at
www.TheInternationalAcademyOfWealth.com/Foundations

Due Diligence Lab

By completing this program, you will be able to:

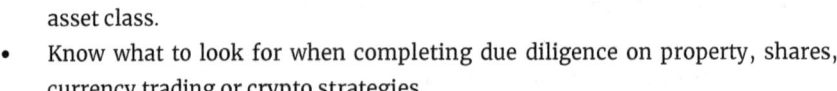

- Understand the importance of due diligence and how it can save you thousands of dollars and hours of stress when implemented correctly.
- Develop your own due diligence action plan to implement when looking at opportunities.
- Understand the different types of due diligence that are required for each asset class.
- Know what to look for when completing due diligence on property, shares, currency trading or crypto strategies.
- Know what questions to ask and when.

Our Due Diligence Lab includes:
- How to complete due diligence basics,
- Advanced due diligence tool kits for property investors,
- Advanced due diligence tool kits for share investors,
- Advanced due diligence tool kits for crypto investors,
- Advanced due diligence tool kits for currency traders,
- Advanced due diligence tool kits for purchasing a business,
- Checklists and action plans,
- Lifetime access and updates.

Join us at
www.TheInternationalAcademyOfWealth.com/DDlabs

The International Academy of Wealth Community Membership

Becoming financially independent requires a lifetime commitment to education. At the Academy, we will provide you with a safe place to learn about wealth creation. A place where like-minded people gather to help lift and encourage others to become the best they can be. Learn about the different types of investment strategies available out there and how and when to add them to your portfolio. Get clear on your goals and how you can achieve them financially.

For more information and complete list of benefits of joining, please join us at the link below.

Join us at
www.TheInternationalAcademyOfWealth.com/application

www.ingramcontent.com/pod-product-compliance
Lightning Source LLC
Chambersburg PA
CBHW072048290426
44110CB00014B/1599